F. W. Lipscomb
Illustrated by John Gardner

A hundred years
of the

AMERICA'S
CUP

HUGH EVELYN LONDON

Respectfully dedicated to
Sir Thomas Sopwith CBE
owner, skipper and sportsman
who so nearly brought the Cup
home to England.

First published in 1971
by Hugh Evelyn Limited
9 Fitzroy Square, London W1P 5AH
The text © 1971, F. W. Lipscomb
The illustrations © 1971, John Gardner
Designed by Norman Reynolds

Printed in Italy by Alfieri & Lacroix

SBN 238.78955.1

Contents

Colour Plates

Acknowledgements

In writing this book I have been greatly helped by a large number of people, too many to include them all by name, and I hope those who are not mentioned will accept my apologies. My special thanks are due to Sir Thomas Sopwith who gave liberally of his time and from whom I received some important and wise advice. I am very grateful to Mr Sohei Holzi, Librarian of the New York Yacht Club, for his prompt replies to requests for information. Also to my friend, William W. Robinson of New York, Editor of *Yachting*, and to Bob Bavier who arranged for facilities for the representative of the publishers to have full use of the Yacht Club, including the model room. My thanks are due to Lloyds Register of Shipping for technical information, including the note on measurements, and to Wing Commander D. I. Fairbairn, British International Measurer, and Mr R. Hollis, Sailing Secretary of the Royal Yachting Association, for guiding me on the subject of fairings and other matters. In order to reproduce accurate drawings of the old courses in New York Harbour and Roads, the Hydrographer of the Navy kindly supplied positions of the marks and buoys concerned.

Of the many people with whom I corresponded, I have to thank Mr E. Christenson of the America's Cup Challenge Syndicate, Sir Frank Packer, Chairman of the Gretel Syndicate, and Mr Alan Payne, designer of *Gretel II*. The most cordial letters, together with photographs, which I have received from Baron Marcel Bich, owner of *France*, have given me great pleasure besides providing all the information I needed. Among those who gave of their time, Miss Nancy Phillips of the Information Department of the United States Embassy, London, was especially helpful.

Finally, I have to express my very sincere thanks to Hugh Street of Hugh Evelyn for his personal help throughout the preparation of the book. Also to Barbara Mills, his assistant, for many hours of proof reading and for cheerfully receiving author's instructions, no matter how difficult the circumstances may have been.

In spite of this help and more from yachting magazines, yacht clubs and yacht builders, I have failed to establish some particulars beyond all doubt. Where this has occurred I have, in agreement with the publishers, written 'not known'. There has been one exception to this, namely, in connection with *Gretel II*. In this case Sir Frank Packer and Mr Alan Payne have individually, both by cable and by letter, informed me that particulars of this twelve metre are being kept confidential and are not yet for publication.

CHAPTER 1

Sparrow-hawk among the Wood-pigeons

The story of the America's Cup races begins in the days when the transition from sail to steam was gathering its greatest momentum. In England, merchants were turning their backs on sail and the cream of commercial sailing ships, the clippers, were being operated by the Americans. This trend spread to the yachtsmen on the other side of the Atlantic and in 1851 an American schooner yacht sailed to England to prove to British yachtsmen that their sailing ships were superior to the English in yachting as well as in commerce.

The sport of yachting had already been enjoyed by the English for at least two centuries. Yachts were owned chiefly by the nobility and the rich gentry. Some clubs had been formed, the most notable being the Royal Yacht Squadron, which was founded in 1815. On the other side of the Atlantic, yachting had been introduced by the English in the colonial days and the sport had soon attracted the Americans. There, too, yacht clubs had sprung up and the most notable of these was the New York Yacht Club, founded in 1844.

Besides the clippers and the yachts, there were in American waters a number of pilot schooners. These sailing ships were famous for their speed, the pilot business being competitive, and pilot schooners often raced in all weathers, as the first to reach the incoming ship took the job.

The renown of these schooners led a group of members of the New York Yacht Club to build the *America* with the idea of showing her in English waters at the time of the Great Trade Fair in 1851. Letters were exchanged between the New York Yacht Club and clubs in England in which the Earl of Wilton, then Commodore of the Royal Yacht Squadron, sent perhaps the most enthusiastic reply. Behind all this lay the excitement of the practice in contemporary yachting circles of cash wagers, sweepstakes and side bets which sometimes reached considerable proportions. The New Yorkers judged their boat would win most of the matches and most of the money.

The first 'syndicate' was made up of six men, Commodore John C. Stevens, Commodore of the New York Yacht Club, his brother, Edwin A. Stevens, George L. Schuyler, Colonel James A. Hamilton, J. Beekman Finley and Hamilton Wilkes.

This syndicate commissioned William H. Brown to build a yacht on pilot boat lines to the design of George Steers, a young designer employed by the firm which had recently designed the pilot schooner *Mary Taylor*, a remarkably fast boat. The syndicate required that if their boat did not prove to be the fastest in the United States or if she was not successful in England they could return her to Brown without payments. Such was the confidence shown in George Steers that Brown accepted these conditions. The yacht Steers designed was 101 feet 9 inches in overall length and 90 feet 3 inches along the waterline. Her beam was 22 feet and she drew 11 feet of water. Her mainmast was 81 feet long, her foremast 79 feet 6 inches and they were well raked when stepped. The bowsprit was 32 feet long and she had a massive main boom, 53 feet long, which extended well over the stern. Her sail plan was simple, a mainsail, a foresail and a single jib with a total area of 5263 square feet. She differed from all that had gone before in almost every aspect of design. Hitherto pilot boats had bluff bows and tapered steadily to the stern, commonly known as 'cod's head and mackerel tail lines', but this time Steers gave his yacht a long

sharp bow with wider sections towards the stern. The rake of her masts enabled the sails to be set better and she carried only one topsail. These features were sufficiently striking in themselves, but apart from this no sails in Britain could compare with the *America*'s. In England sails were still made of flax, but in America yachtsmen had begun to make their sails of machined cotton. British sails were baggy and were kept flat by drenching the luffs with water. The *America*'s sails, made by R. H. Wilson of New York, set more taut and she carried two very large headsails which she could set when conditions were favourable and which did most of the work, a practice which has been fully developed in recent years with immense success. Both foresail and mainsail were laced to booms. Such were all the experiments incorporated in one yacht that she turned out to be a very fast vessel indeed. Her deck was of yellow pine $2\frac{1}{2}$ inches thick and her wooden hull was planked with white oak 3 inches thick. She was copper fastened throughout and copper sheathed from her keel to 6 inches above the waterline. She was rated 170 tons by Custom House measurement* and carried 45 tons of ballast all inboard. Between decks she was fitted out very much on the lines of the standard pilot cutters, with accommodation which was comfortable for fifteen men.

On completion the *America* carried out a few trial races against a fast centreboard sloop, built for racing along the American coast, and a handful of other types. She did not beat the 'skimming dish', as the centreboard sloop was called, but the syndicate were satisfied and on 21 June 1851 she sailed for Le Havre, where she arrived 20 days later and proceeded to fit out for the testing days which lay ahead.

On 31 July the *America* sailed for Cowes, but the weather was against her and she was delayed showing herself off the Royal Yacht Squadron Club House by having to anchor some six miles away and wait for the dawn. This gave an enterprising English yachtsman the opportunity of going to meet the Americans when they weighed anchor to beat up to Cowes the next morning. Commodore Stevens, who was on board the *America*, could have put up a cruising rig and kept the boat's speed a secret but he was a good sportsman and accepted the challenge. Almost within minutes of being under weigh it was clear that the *America* was a very fast yacht and this news speedily reached many yachtsmen of note in England. When Commodore Stevens tried to arrange a match with any British yacht there were no 'takers'. Apart from this initial disappointment it looked as though the financial aspect of the venture could be in jeopardy. A caustic comment appeared in *The Times*, which read:

'Most of us have seen the agitation which the
appearance of a sparrow-hawk on the horizon
invokes among a flock of wood-pigeons or sky-
larks when they all at once come down to the

---

* Three types of measurements are mentioned in the text. They are technical rather than of general interest. In broad terms they deal with length, breadth and depth and are taken from various specific points on the deck and in the hull. Custom House measurements are used by the Customs and are primarily concerned with displacement. Thames measurements are more generally used in yachting circles and are concerned with rating and handicapping. Universal measurements have been employed for various purposes more in America than anywhere else but are no longer in use.

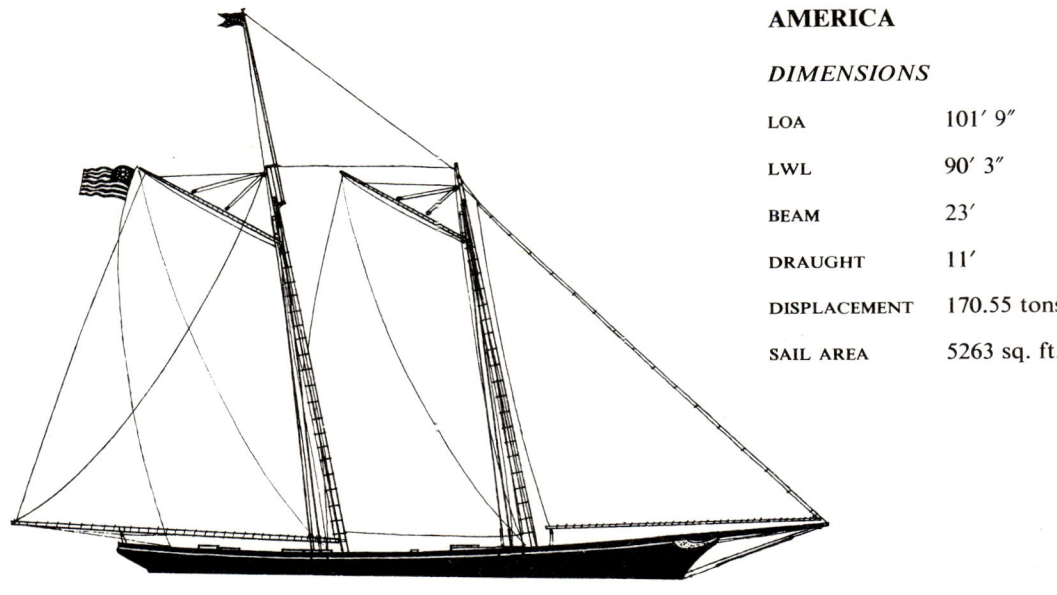

AMERICA

DIMENSIONS

LOA	101′ 9″
LWL	90′ 3″
BEAM	23′
DRAUGHT	11′
DISPLACEMENT	170.55 tons
SAIL AREA	5263 sq. ft.

SERIES	DATE	NAME (winners name first)	COURSE	ELAPSED TIME	CORRECTED TIME	WINS BY	REMARKS
	August 22 1851	*AMERICA* *AURORA*	Around the Isle of Wight starting from the Royal Yacht Squadron Club at Cowes *58 miles*	10.37.00 10.45.00		8m 00s	*AURORA* *came second*

ground and are rendered almost motionless for fear of the disagreeable visitor. Although the gentlemen whose business is on the waters of the Solent are neither wood-pigeons nor skylarks, and although the America *is not a sparrow-hawk, the offset produced by her apparition off West Cowes among yachtsmen seems to have been completely paralysing. She has flung down the gauntlet to England, Ireland and Scotland and not one has been found there to take it up.'*

This embarrassing situation was relieved by the Royal Yacht Squadron informing Commodore Stevens that there would be a race for 'all comers' round the Isle of Wight for a cup to be won outright valued at a hundred guineas, on 22 August, and the *America* would be welcome to come in on it. Many yachtsmen thought that this was only adding further embarrassment, as half the course would be in enclosed waters where local knowledge would be vital. To have to sail under this handicap against a whole fleet of yachts was beyond the limit of bad manners from a host to a guest. However the *America* turned up at the starting line and anchored, as was the custom in those days. She found seventeen British cutters and schooners in the line, ranging from the 47-ton cutter *Aurora* to the three-masted schooner *Brilliant* of 392 tons. Thus the *America* was about middle size in this fleet of the cream of British yachts.

When the starting gun went off the *America* had some difficulty with her anchor gear and got away last of all, but by the time she reached the Nab she had run through the whole fleet except four; they were *Beatrice*, *Aurora*, *Volante* and *Arrow* which were keeping close together so that the *America* had to alter course constantly to try and pass but invariably found her way blocked. All this was on a run, the wind being in the west, but once the yachts turned for the beat to St Catherine's Point the *America* raced through them and, on rounding the Point, there was not another yacht in sight. Unfortunately the *Arrow*, one of the fastest cutters of the home side, had gone aground and the *Alarm*, another particularly good yacht, had withdrawn to stand by her. By this time, however, the easterly tide had begun to run and the little 47-ton *Aurora* came on the scene once again. But it was not to last, for the wind freshened and the *America* raced to the Needles at 14 knots; some said she was nearly 8 miles ahead.

The finish of the race is well known. Queen Victoria's interest in the race had led her to be present at the finishing line in the Royal Yacht. As soon as the *America* had crossed the line, so the story goes, Her Majesty asked the Yeoman of Signals who would be second. 'There is no second', was the reply. In fact the *Aurora* did come in second being only two miles astern when the *America* finished.

So the hundred-guinea cup went to the *America* and although English yachtsmen asked their guests to remain while a yacht was built which they said would beat her, the money offered for the race was too small to make a prolonged stay by the Americans in English waters acceptable. This financial aspect was even more emphasised since the crew of the *America*

could obtain no bets on any match which was suggested.

One more race was eventually arranged, this time against a single yacht, the *Titania*. The course was a simple one – 20 miles to windward and return, the starting point being the Nab lightship, just east of the Isle of Wight. This race did more to influence future yacht design than any previous contest. The *America*'s greatest-pulling headsails enabled her to race ahead of the *Titania* into the head sea. At no time was the result in doubt and she won by 52 minutes in spite of carrying away her fore gaff.

The subsequent history of this remarkable yacht was most varied. First, Lord John de Blaguiere purchased her and immediately altered her masts. As a result of this she lost her racing trim and English helmsmen did not seem able, at this stage, to get the best out of the flat sails. Having changed hands once more, in England, and altered her name to *Camilla* she was bought by an American for the Confederates. She had a few guns mounted and operated as a dispatch boat until a Yankee gun-boat chased her up the St John's River, where she scuttled. The Federals then raised her and she fought on their side until in 1864 she was sent to the Marine Academy at Annapolis for use as a training ship. This was by no means her last resting place. The government sold her to General Butler of Massachusetts, in whose family she remained until 1916, and during this period she appeared in the first Cup race in 1870 and in the first Canadian Challenge in 1876 and later off Sandy Hook where a party on her deck watched the *Vigilant/Valkyrie* Match. From 1916 to 1921 she lay at Boston, where she was bought by a group of yachtsmen who refitted her and presented her to the U.S. Naval Academy. Unfortunately the U.S. Navy could obtain no government grant to maintain her and throughout the Second World War she was lying out of the water at Annapolis.

With the end of the war, in 1945, she was broken up but never forgotten. It is fair to say that the *America*, apart from the cup and all it has come to mean in international yachting, was the forerunner of the thinking which guides all marine yacht design today, in respect of both the hull and the sails.

So the only thing Commodore Stevens took home with him was the hundred-guinea Cup. It was not a thing of great beauty, more like a large pitcher that has no bottom to it, so the holder cannot drink out of it. It is housed today in a separate room in the New York Yacht Club. This room is circular, so one can walk round the cup, which stands on a plinth in a glass case. Before entering this room one feels like a visitor to a Buddhist shrine and the inclination is to take one's shoes off. Today it signifies all that goes into the sport of yachting and no one has calculated the total amount of money which has been spent in competing for it, but it has been prodigious. All the same, by its existence and the terms under which it is open to competition, this Cup has contributed more than anything else to the advancement of design in marine architecture, and of the skills in weaving sails.

The hundred-guinea cup was the property of the syndicate which built the *America* and they decided that it should remain in the custody of Commodore Stevens who took it to his house in Washington. There it remained until 1857 when Commodore Stevens, together with the four surviving members of the original syndicate, handed it over to the New

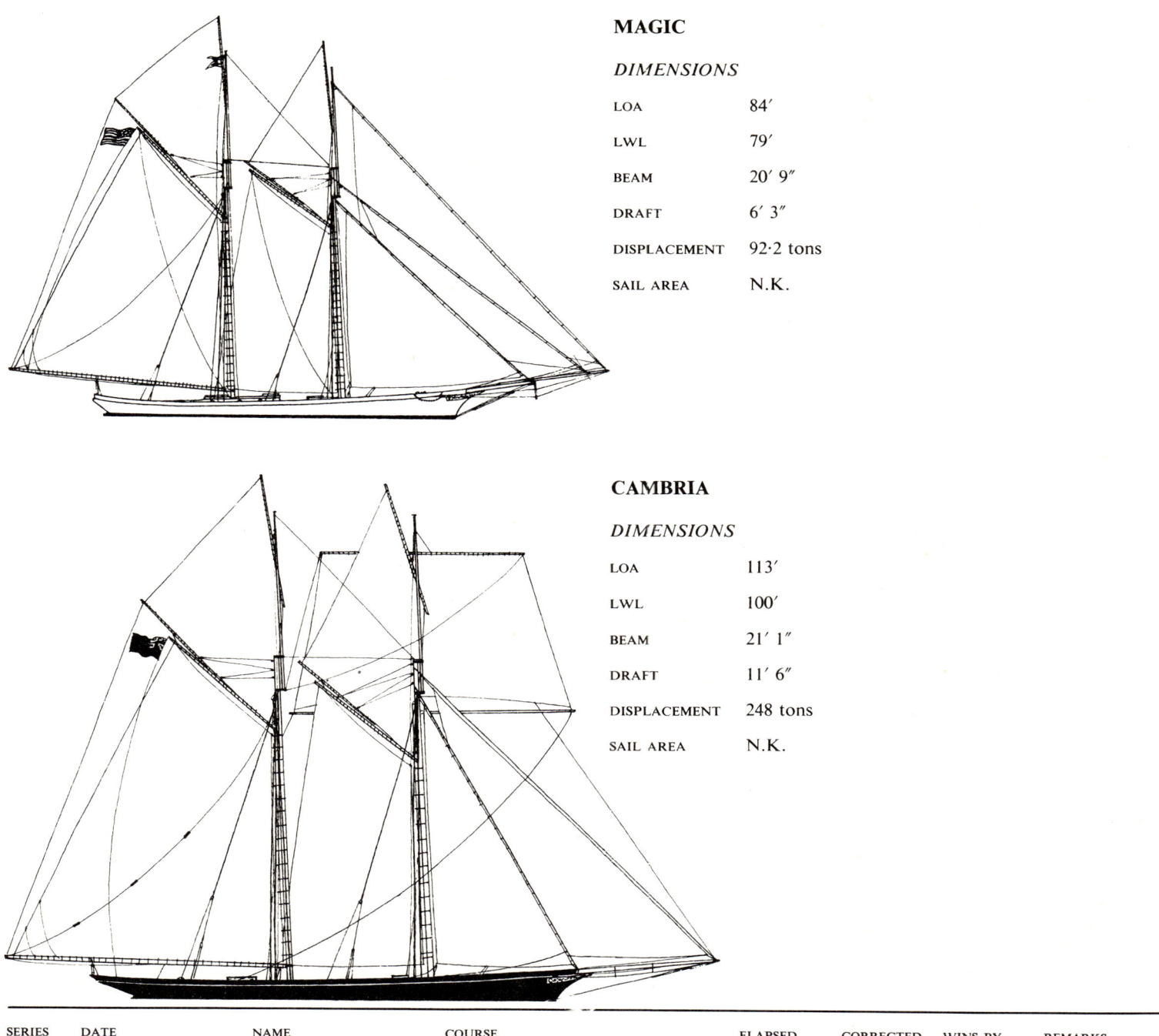

MAGIC

DIMENSIONS

LOA	84'
LWL	79'
BEAM	20' 9"
DRAFT	6' 3"
DISPLACEMENT	92·2 tons
SAIL AREA	N.K.

CAMBRIA

DIMENSIONS

LOA	113'
LWL	100'
BEAM	21' 1"
DRAFT	11' 6"
DISPLACEMENT	248 tons
SAIL AREA	N.K.

SERIES	DATE	NAME (winners name first)	COURSE	ELAPSED TIME	CORRECTED TIME	WINS BY	REMARKS
1st	August 8 1870	*MAGIC* *CAMBRIA*	New York Yacht Club Course *35·1 miles*	4.07.54 4.34.57	3.58.21·2 4.37.38·9	39m 17·7s	*CAMBRIA came tenth*

York Yacht Club, to be held as a permanent challenge cup on international level.

Conditions of Trust were drawn up as follows:

1. Any organised yacht club of any foreign country shall be entitled, through any one or more of its members, to claim the right of sailing a match for the Cup.
2. Any match can be made by mutual consent, but if this cannot be agreed, then the course shall be the usual course for the annual regatta of the defending club.
3. Yachts must be not less than 30 tons or more than 300 tons, Custom House measurement of the country to which the yacht belongs.
4. Six months' notice in writing must be given, together with a day named for the start.
5. The cup is to be the property of the club and not the member or members thereof.

The letter giving these terms in full was dated 8 July 1857, and signed by:

J. C. Stevens
Edwin A. Steers
Hamilton Wilkes
J. Beekman Finley
George L. Schuyler

The scene was now set for the greatest challenge cup in the history of yachting and inevitably the trophy became known as the 'America's Cup'.

But nothing happened for a very long time – indeed, not until 1868, by which time the existence of the cup had almost been forgotten, when a letter arrived at the New York Yacht Club from Mr James Ashbury of England, owner of the schooner *Cambria*.

Mr Ashbury had complete faith in his *Cambria* by reason of the fact that in 1868 a large American schooner, the *Sappho*, had come over to England and in a race around the Isle of Wight his yacht had beaten the American easily. Later he was further encouraged as he arranged to sail the *Cambria* over to America in competition with the *Dauntless*, the property of James Gordon Bennett, Vice-Commodore of the New York Yacht Club. This race started on 4 July 1870 and Mr Ashbury won it to the dismay of all American yachtsmen. Actually they need not have been too disheartened because the *Dauntless* led nearly all the way and the *Cambria* found a lucky breeze during the last 24 hours which carried her away from her rival.

From 1868 to the summer of 1870 Mr Ashbury had carried on a lengthy correspondence with the New York Yacht Club. In this he had made a number of proposals, the majority of which were not within the terms of the trust governing competitors for the America's Cup. In the end, there being no agreement by mutual consent, the Americans gave *Cambria*'s owner the option of sailing for the America's Cup in one race over the Club's regular course, a distance of 38 miles, but against the Club fleet. This latter condition was believed to be the correct interpretation of the terms of the trust, but it gave an enormous advantage to the defending club although, as some yachtsmen pointed out, the *America* had sailed

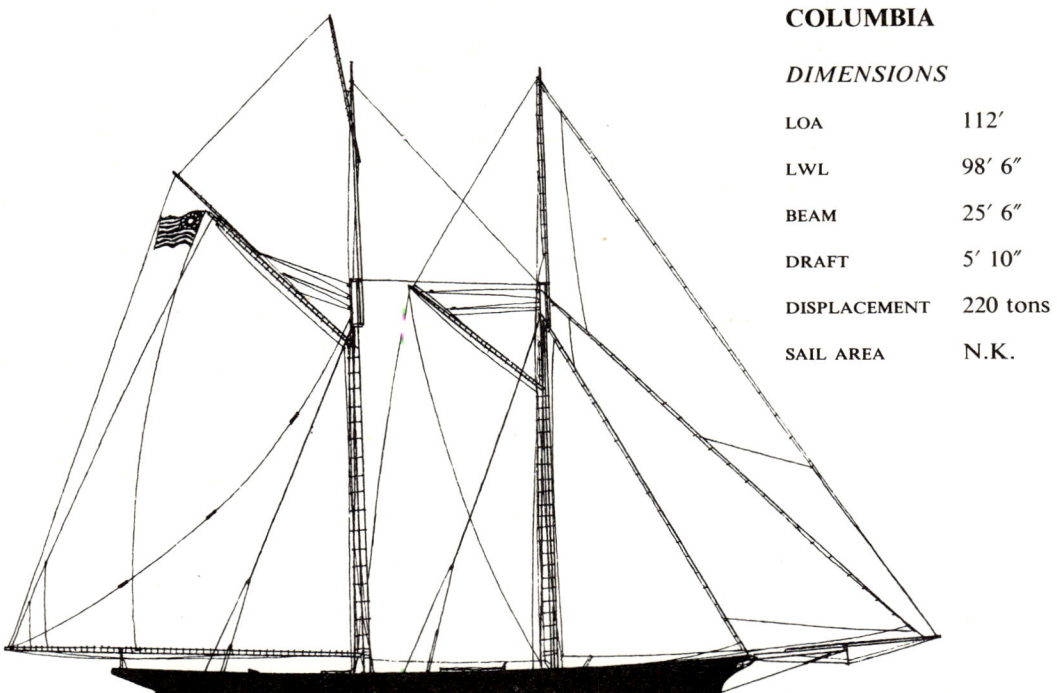

COLUMBIA

DIMENSIONS

LOA	112′
LWL	98′ 6″
BEAM	25′ 6″
DRAFT	5′ 10″
DISPLACEMENT	220 tons
SAIL AREA	N.K.

SERIES	DATE	NAME (winners name first)	COURSE	ELAPSED TIME	CORRECTED TIME	WINS BY	REMARKS
2nd Part I	October 16 1871	*COLUMBIA* *LIVONIA*	New York Yacht Club Course *35·1 miles*	6.17.42 6.43.00	6.19.41 6.46.45	27m 04s	
2nd Part I	October 18 1871	*COLUMBIA* *LIVONIA*	20 miles to windward from Sandy Hook Lightship and return *40 miles*	3.01.33·5 3.06.49·5	3.07.41·7 3.18.15·5	10m 33s	
2nd Part 1	October 19 1871	*LIVONIA* *COLUMBIA*	New York Yacht Club Course *35·1 miles*	3.53.05 4.12.38	4.02.25 4.17.35	15m 10s	*COLUMBIA partially disabled*

against the crack fleet of the Royal Yacht Squadron. There was already talk of the handicap which the challenger had to suffer through having to sail across the Atlantic 'on her own bottom'. This latter condition was perhaps the more exacting of the two since there had been developed, on the eastern seaboard of the United States, some centreboard yachts with shallow, broad hulls. These yachts could 'skim' along and would never have been put to the test of an Atlantic crossing. Yachts with 'plates' or yachts with 'keels' has been the subject of discussion ever since this first challenge, and understandably the owner and crew of the *Cambria* were upset with what they considered to be unjust terms. Rather than have no race at all, Mr Ashbury accepted the terms and the race was organised for 8 August. *Cambria* was a wooden schooner of 193 tons Thames measurement and had been built by Ratsey of Cowes in 1868 to the design of the builder. She was 120 feet long overall and, like the *America* before her, copper-fastened and copper-sheathed.

Twenty-three boats came out to sail against the *Cambria*. This time they were sailing solely to keep the Cup in the United States, as the winner had no right to the Cup at all. There were seven keel schooners, including the *America*, and sixteen centreboarders. Public interest was immense, Wall Street and Broad Street finance houses closed and people flocked to sea to witness the start, many of whom had never set foot on a yacht before. The course was the standard New York Yacht Club course of 35.1 miles. *Magic* was first away but *Cambria* did well enough and got a good position. It was a beat out to the Sandy Hook light vessel and the little *Magic* took every advantage of local knowledge, but *Cambria* in any case was never in the running to win. Indeed, the *America* rounded the light ship second, showing once again how these big headsails could pull when working to windward in favourable conditions. The return to the spit buoy was a broad reach and all the yachts put up every sail they dared. *Cambria* dared too much and carried away her fore topmast, but she went on and ran home, finishing in tenth place, while the *America* came romping home ahead of her in fourth place. Mr Ashbury took his defeat in good heart and was liberally entertained, but all agreed that no more races for the Cup should be held with a fleet of yachts from the country holding the trophy.

There was a postscript to this first of all the challenges. After much correspondence Mr Ashbury arranged with the New York Yacht Club that if he challenged again he would race against one yacht only. This was agreed, but the Americans reserved the right to choose any yacht they

thought suited to the prevailing conditions on the day. Naturally, this was still felt to be unfair to the challenger, and in addition, Mr Ashbury's request that such yachts should be keel boats like his, and not centre-boarders, was also turned down. Nevertheless, he took over a new yacht in 1871, the *Livonia*, racing over the New York Yacht Club course first against *Columbia*, a centreboarder, and then against the more familiar *Sappho*, a keel yacht. He won the race against *Columbia*, who carried away her jib stay and then her steering gear, but lost the next two against *Sappho*. The series ended with much misunderstanding on both sides and loss of civility on the part of Mr Ashbury which engendered a good deal of ill-feeling between the two countries but, on the plus side, it paved the way to fairer rules and better contests in the future.

Livonia was another schooner, built by Ratsey at Cowes. With her two masts she carried an immense sail area of over 18,000 square feet with a hull of 115-foot length. She was a particularly fine example of schooners then building in European waters. There was considerable professional disappointment in English yachting circles when *Livonia* was beaten by the keel yacht *Sappho*, showing that the Americans could build this type better than most people had forecast when *Livonia* went across the Atlantic.

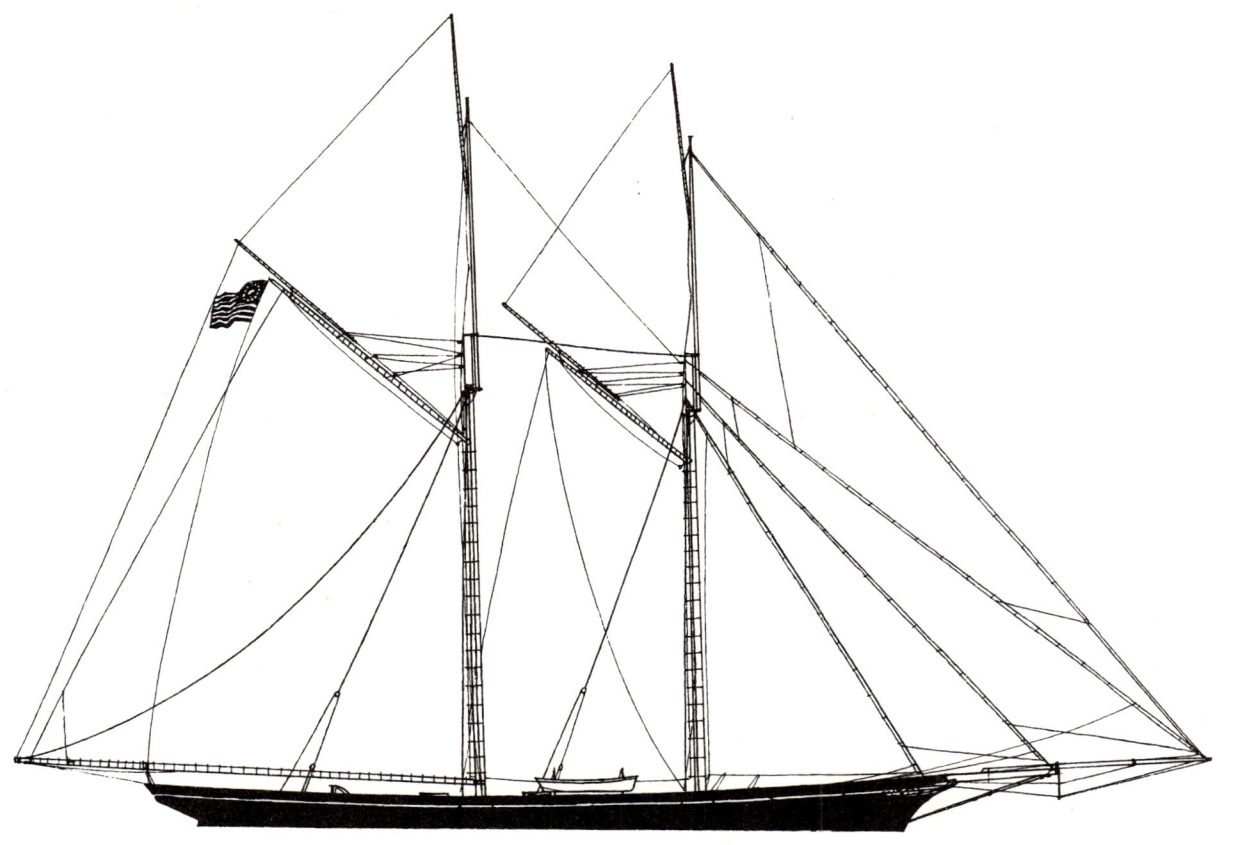

SAPPHO

DIMENSIONS

LOA	138'
LWL	121'
BEAM	27'
DRAFT	12' 10"
DISPLACEMENT	310 tons
SAIL AREA	N.K.

LIVONIA

DIMENSIONS

LOA	127'
LWL	106'
BEAM	23' 7".
DRAFT	12' 6"
DISPLACEMENT	264 tons
SAIL AREA	N.K.

SERIES	DATE	NAME (winners name first)	COURSE	ELAPSED TIME	CORRECTED TIME	WINS BY	REMARKS
2nd Part II	October 21 1871	SAPPHO LIVONIA	20 miles to windward from Sandy Hook Lightship and return 40 miles	5.33.24 6.04.38	5.36.02 6.09.23	33m 21s	
2nd Part II	October 23 1871	SAPPHO LIVONIA	New York Yacht Club Course 40 miles	4.38.05 5.04.41	4.46.17 5.11.44	25m 27s	

CHAPTER 2

Canadian Challenge

It was not for over a decade that an English yacht club took up this challenge again, partly due to the difficult conditions in the Deed of Gift but also in no small measure to the coldness between the two countries following Mr Ashbury's efforts, both with the pen and in his relationship with the New York Yacht Club, who followed up his departure by returning three cups he had presented to the Club.

The gap was filled by the Canadians with two challenges which ended in no better feeling than in the case of Mr Ashbury.

Yachting in the Great Lakes was of a high standard and in the conditions many yachtsmen raced centreboarders. Americans came across the border and at times 'cleaned up' the best cups with new yachts and progressive ideas. So the Canadians were well equipped in experience and knowledge of their prospective opponents.

The first challenge was made in 1881 by the Royal Canadian Yacht Club with a yacht called *Countess of Dufferin* which was owned by a syndicate, the principal member of which was a Major Charles Gifford, the Vice-Commodore of the Club. At the request of the challenger the six-month clause was waived and the challenge accepted. The Canadian yacht had been designed and built by Alexander Cuthbert who had recently produced a yacht which had beaten one of the American 'flyers' on the lakes. The Americans, however, had a winner in their schooner *Madeleine* and there was no question in their choice which, as a result of correspondence and much sportsmanship on the part of the Committee of the New York Yacht Club, was to be the only yacht defending. This was another departure of some magnitude from their rights by the Deed to sail any yacht of their choosing according to the conditions on the day.

The Canadians came round to New York by way of the St Lawrence River and the open sea and at first sight the *Countess* looked a good yacht, but it was soon clear on closer viewing that money had been short. Not only was her hull rough but her sails were not up to international standards. Although much was done at the last minute to rectify this, the result of the races was never in doubt. Not only did the *Madeleine* win the first two by large margins, but in the second race the old *America* turned up and sailed over the course, although not in the contest, and beat the challenger by 19 minutes 9 seconds. A sea mark was used for starting this race, and this was the first time that the start was not made from anchor. This challenge also marked the end of the schooners in America's Cup racing.*

Cuthbert was not dismayed with the result of the racing. He now belonged to the Bay of Quinti Yacht Club and on 16 May 1881 the Club sent a challenge on his behalf. Once again the New York Yacht Club agreed to waive the six months' notice and also agreed to race only one yacht and the same one for all races. The challenger was a centreboard sloop designed and built by Cuthbert on the lines of a successful sloop, the *Annie Cuthbert*. This new yacht was called *Atalanta*. The Americans took the challenge most seriously and commissioned David Kirby, the builder of *Madeleine*, to build a boat specially to defend the Cup. This was the

---

* Schooners are yachts with two or more masts rigged fore and aft; cutters are single-masted yachts with two or more headsails; sloops are single-masted yachts with a single headsail. In America all single-masted yachts regardless of sail plan can be called sloops.

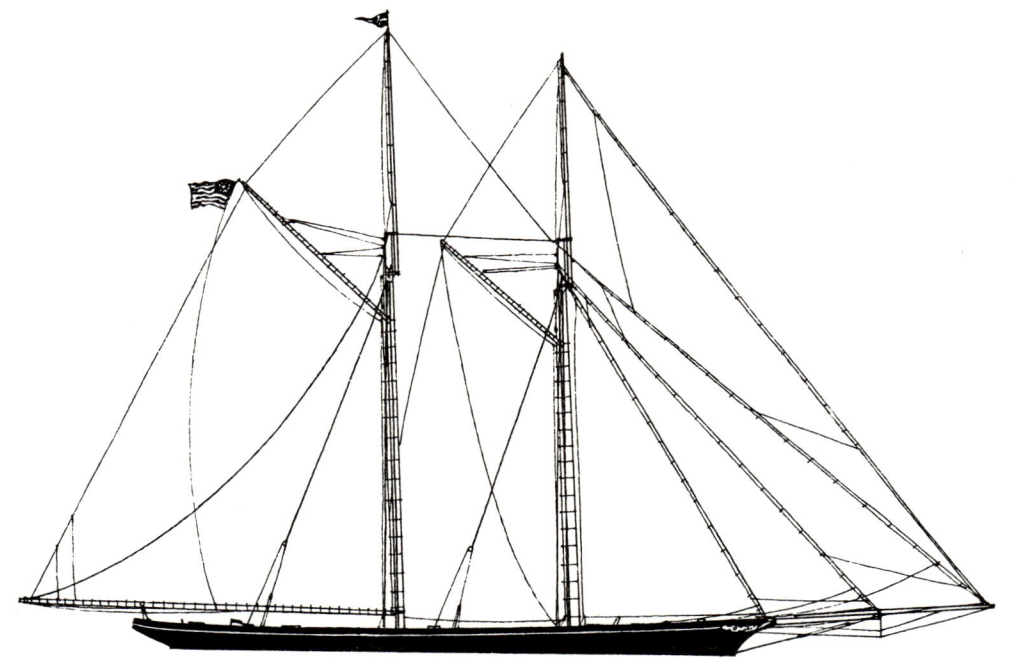

MADELEINE

DIMENSIONS

LOA	106'
LWL	91'
BEAM	24'
DRAFT	7' 5"
DISPLACEMENT	151·49 tons
SAIL AREA	N.K.

COUNTESS OF DUFFERIN

DIMENSIONS

LOA	107'
LWL	95'
BEAM	24'
DRAFT	6' 6"
DISPLACEMENT	138·20 tons
SAIL AREA	N.K.

SERIES	DATE	NAME (winners name first)	COURSE	ELAPSED TIME	CORRECTED TIME	WINS BY	REMARKS
3rd	August 11 1876	*MADELEINE*	New York Yacht Club Course	5.24.55	5.23.54	10m 59s	
		COUNTESS OF DUFFERIN	*32·6 miles*	5.34.53	5.34.53		
3rd	August 12 1876	*MADELEINE*	20 miles to windward from Sandy	7.19.47	7.18.46	27m 14s	
		COUNTESS OF DUFFERIN	Hook Lightship and return *40 miles*	7.46.00	7.46.00		

first time this had been done and it ushered in a long line of yachts all specially built by the Americans to defend. Kirby built the *Pocahontas*, guaranteed, as he said, to beat the *Arrow*, his best so far. Then again, for the first time, the Americans decided to have trials to choose the defender, so the *Pocahontas* raced against five other crack sloops and was beaten by the *Mischief*. The winner was an iron centreboard sloop with lines which were a compromise between the 'skimming dish' design and the keel boats.

Cuthbert meanwhile was bringing his boat through the Erie Canal instead of the St Lawrence River and ocean route. The yacht had to be heeled over to get her through some of the locks, which were only six feet deep. This news offended the defender and rightly so. Cuthbert sailed his boat with a largely amateur crew rather poorly trained. When the racing began it was immediately clear that the challenger was no match at all for the defender and the series took place virtually without interest, the *Mischief* winning the first races easily.

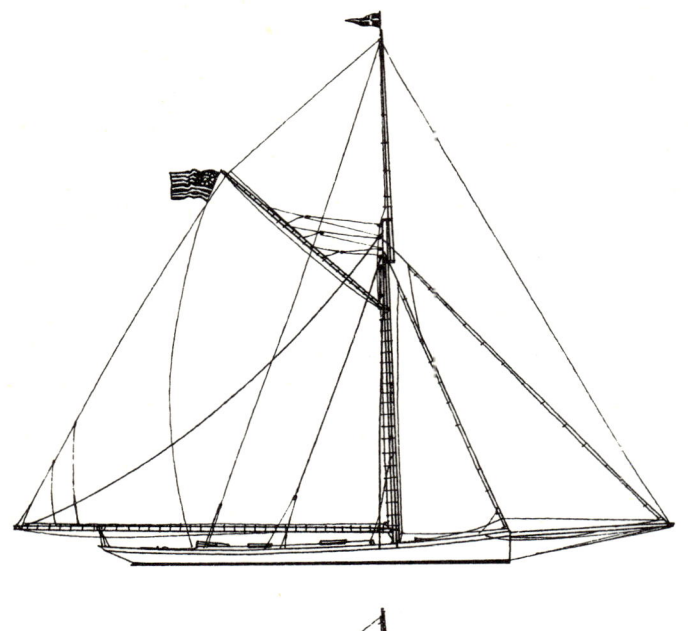

MISCHIEF

DIMENSIONS

LOA	68' 6"
LWL	61'
BEAM	19' 11"
DRAFT	5' 8"
DISPLACEMENT	79·27 tons
SAIL AREA	N.K.

ATALANTA

DIMENSIONS

LOA	71'
LWL	63' 10"
BEAM	19' 2"
DRAFT	5' 5"
DISPLACEMENT	84 tons
SAIL AREA	N.K.

SERIES	DATE	NAME (winners name first)	COURSE	ELAPSED TIME	CORRECTED TIME	WINS BY	REMARKS
4th	November 9 1881	*MISCHIEF* *ATALANTA*	New York Yacht Club Course *32·6 miles*	4.17.09 4.48.24·5	4.17.09 4.45.29·25	28m 20·25s	
4th	November 10 1881	*MISCHIEF* *ATALANTA*	16 miles to leeward from Buoy No. 5 off Sandy Hook and return *32 miles*	4.54.53 5.36.52	4.54.53 5.33.47	38m 54s	

As a result of this contest yachtsmen all over the world felt that the spirit of the America's Cup, as visualised by the founder of the competition, had been flouted. Towing the challenger by mule through the canal was against the whole basis of the originator's ideas, namely that foreign yachts should cross the seas on 'their own bottoms' to fetch the Cup. In short, the terms and conditions of the competition had got into a mess, so the New York Yacht Club, finding that one member of the original syndicate was still alive, namely Mr George L. Schuyler, returned the Cup to him and asked him to draw up a new Deed of Gift.

CHAPTER 3

The *Genesta* Challenge and the Dunraven Affair

The next British challenge was made by Sir Richard Sutton who owned the cutter *Genesta*, a most interesting yacht. She was an extreme type of keel boat being 90 feet 6 inches in length overall but with a beam of only 15 feet. For good measure she carried over 7000 square feet of sail. People referred to her as 'the plank on edge'. She was kept upright by a massive keel weighing 70 tons. Nearly all American boats, centreboard or keel, were beamy, and *Genesta* appeared to them as something beyond their comprehension. The designer was J. Beavor-Webb.

Mr George L. Schuyler meanwhile had drawn up a new Deed of Gift and had returned the Cup to the New York Yacht Club. The new Deed of Gift, which was accepted by the Club, more or less confirmed the terms and conditions which had come into use over the years. Briefly they were that the Club holding the Cup must meet the challenge with one yacht only. The challenger must sail on her own bottom to the scene of the contest. A yacht once defeated could not challenge again for two years. The 'match' must be a matter of mutual consent as regards course and number of races. There must be six months' notice of a challenge. There was an extra clause, which incensed the Canadians, that if any of their clubs challenged again the club must be situated on the seaboard of the Dominion. A great many pretty hard things were said about this in the Canadian papers, but yachtsmen generally throughout the world were agreed that the high principles which the original syndicate drew up for the contests were fundamental to its place in international racing and the new Deed upheld these.

There was some discussion on a further point of importance, namely the system of time allowances. This was referred back to the donor who said 'the time allowance should be made in accordance with the rules of the club in possession'.*

Once again a syndicate was formed from members of the New York Yacht Club who astonished many an old hand by commissioning a comparatively young man, Edward Burgess, who had never built a large sloop before, to design the defender. The result was the *Puritan*. This yacht was almost entirely of the opposite school to the 'plank on edge'. She was wide and drew only 8 feet, but with her centreboard down her draught was 20 feet. Here was a true test of the two schools of thought, the broad centreboard and the 'plank on edge'.

The 7th September was set for the first of the three races to be sailed by mutual consent. Before this, both yachts had been hoisted out of the water. The *Genesta*'s coppered under-body had been polished by hand until it was like a looking glass and the *Puritan*'s had been potleaded so that it was as slippery as an eel.

Fog eventually caused the postponement of the first race until the following day and then, when the yachts were manoeuvring for the start, *Puritan*'s skipper failed to respond to a luff by *Genesta*, who had the right of way, and *Genesta*'s bowsprit went clean through *Puritan*'s mainsail. The Committee immediately sent word that *Puritan* had been disqualified and informed Sir Richard Sutton that if he sailed over the course the race

---

* A detailed explanation of handicapping has been purposely omitted since most readers would find it tedious while the expert would require more information than there is space for.

would be awarded to him. However, this time England had sent over a true sportsman who declared that he had come over for a race and not a walkover.

It was 11 September before both boats had been repaired and on this day there was very little wind and it became clear after five hours racing that neither yacht would finish within the seven hour limit. The next race was 14 September and everything seemed set for a good race. There was a fair south-west breeze and the course was from off Owl's Head to Sandy Hook light vessel and back – 38 miles in all. *Puritan* got the better of the start and as the two yachts, followed by the ever more numerous spectator fleet, made their way through the narrows where they had to tack, *Genesta* was bothered by an incoming barque and by the time they reached the open sea *Puritan* was seven minutes ahead, but here the wind became fluky and *Genesta* reduced the lead to three minutes at the South West Spit buoy. It was a reach to the light vessel and here *Puritan* gained a minute or so, partly because excursion boats again hampered *Genesta*. On the run back, the flat-bottomed boat did better, as might be expected, and the latter part of the race was devoid of excitement as the wind dropped away and *Puritan* steadily drew ahead, finishing sixteen minutes and nineteen seconds ahead on corrected time.

The second race, sailed on the 16th, was one of the best of all America's Cup contests. This time the start was a run and *Genesta* got away first. It was all set for the 'plank on edge' and half way to the light vessel there seemed no hope for the defender. At the mark the wind freshened and all *Genesta* had to do was beat it home, but for reasons never fully understood Captain Carter set his gaff topsail, while *Puritan*, judging the wind too strong for a topsail, housed her topmast. From that moment *Puritan* steadily gained and finally shot over the finishing line with a glorious stern wake, two minutes ahead of the challenger.

It had been a tremendous race. Both crews cheered each other and the spectator fleet – those which had been able to keep up with the competitors – had had a magnificent day. England lost because *Genesta* made the mistake of cramming on too much canvas, a lesson which is still being learned today even by experienced yachtsmen.

There followed in 1886 a challenge by the Royal Northern Yacht Club of Scotland on behalf of Lieutenant William Henn who owned *Galatea*. This yacht was also designed by J. Beavor-Webb who had designed *Genesta*. She was built of steel, the first challenger to be so constructed, and was nicknamed 'the steel frigate', although some people called her 'the lead mine' as she had 81 tons of this metal in her keel.

The defender was *Mayflower* and Captain 'Hank' Haff was selected to sail her. The name of 'Hank' Haff is well known to those who have studied the America's Cup story. All that need be said of this race was that *Mayflower* won with considerable ease.

This match could have been particularly interesting as *Mayflower* was built by Edward Burgess. In him and Beavor-Webb were the two most brilliant designers on either side of the Atlantic, but *Galatea* was not prepared for the battle. Lieutenant Henn was a retired naval officer who retired on board his yacht with his wife and it was fitted out accordingly. His chances against a yacht virtually stripped of all extra fittings, a feature which was being closely studied for the first time at this period, coupled

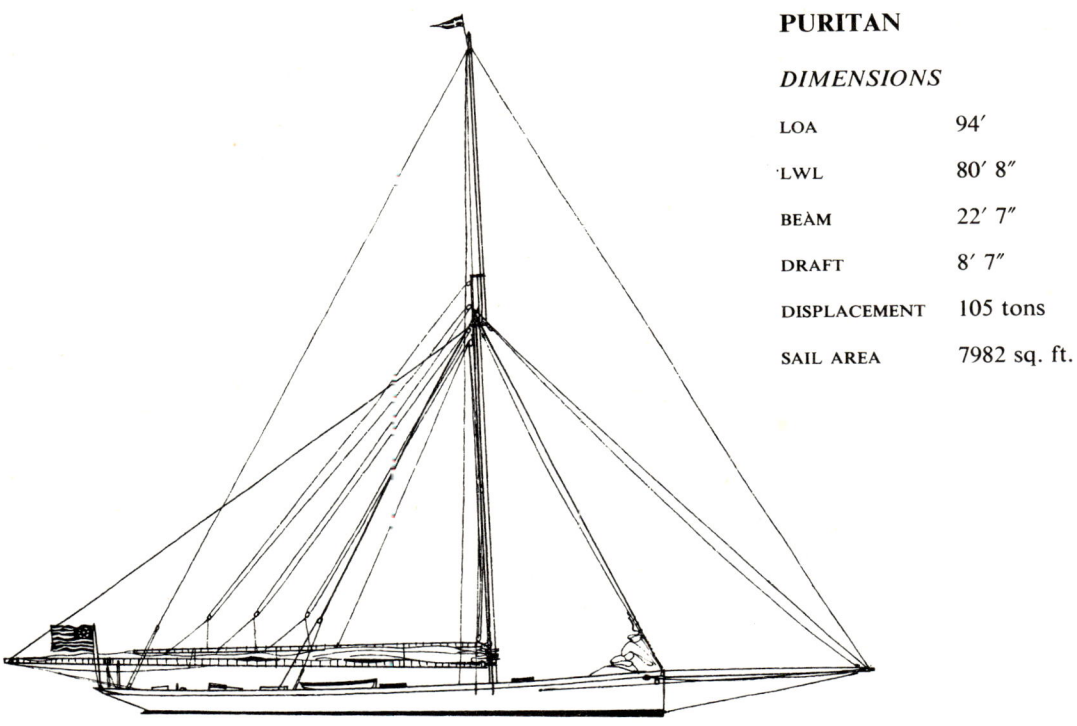

PURITAN

DIMENSIONS

LOA	94'
LWL	80' 8"
BEAM	22' 7"
DRAFT	8' 7"
DISPLACEMENT	105 tons
SAIL AREA	7982 sq. ft.

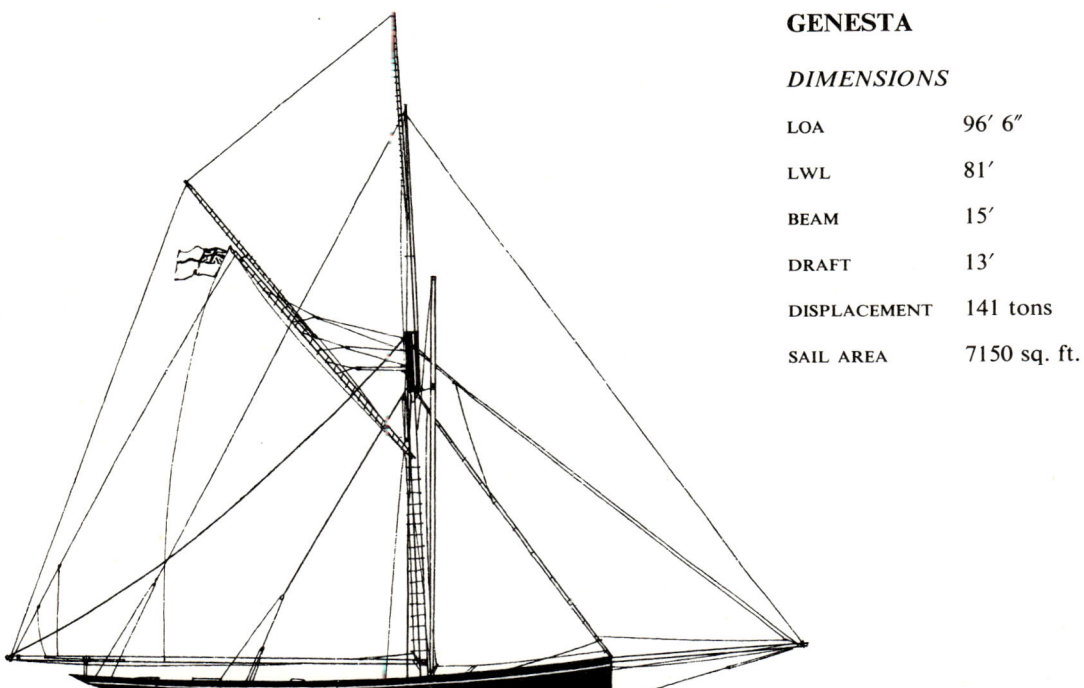

GENESTA

DIMENSIONS

LOA	96' 6"
LWL	81'
BEAM	15'
DRAFT	13'
DISPLACEMENT	141 tons
SAIL AREA	7150 sq. ft.

SERIES	DATE	NAME (winners name first)	COURSE	ELAPSED TIME	CORRECTED TIME	WINS BY	REMARKS
5th	September 14 1885	PURITAN GENESTA	New York Yacht Club Course 32·6 miles	6.06.05 6.22.52	6.06.05 6.22.54	16m 49s	
5th	September 16 1885	PURITAN GENESTA	20 miles to leeward from Sandy Hook Lightship and return 40 miles	5.03.14 5.05.20	5.03.14 5.04.52	1m 38s	

with having to sail against 'Hank' Haff, were never worth considering.

Not long after this series a letter was received by the New York Yacht Club from Scotland. In this the Royal Clyde Yacht Club proposed a contest in 1887 on behalf of Mr James Bell. As the prevailing Deed of Gift stipulated at least six months' notice but not over seven months, the New York Yacht Club said they would consider the matter when it came in proper form. Bell was not to be put off. He formed a syndicate and commissioned George L. Watson to design a yacht. She was built in Glasgow that winter and Bell sent his formal challenge in March 1887. The yacht was named *Thistle* and brought to the fore the name of G. L. Watson, one of the great designers of America's Cup challengers.

The defender was built in quick time by Pusey and Jones of Wilmington, Delaware, to the order of General Charles J. Paine. She was christened *Volunteer*.

The racing started on 27 September 1887 with much speculation on both sides of the Atlantic, as both yachts had done remarkably well in races that summer. The agreement was to have three races, one over the inside course and two 'out and back' from the Sandy Hook light vessel. *Volunteer* won the first two races by over ten minutes.

Bell and his Scottish team were overcome with disappointment. They could not understand how their yacht had done so badly but perhaps there was not so much difference in the yachts. Local knowledge and 'Hank' Haff at the helm of *Volunteer* probably accounted for a good deal.

'Hank' Haff was still going strong nearly a decade later and took part in what is sometimes called 'the Dunraven Affair'. The noble Earl had already challenged once in 1893 with his *Valkyrie II* built by G. L. Watson, but had been faced with sailing against a yacht, the *Vigilant*, built by one of the greatest designers, Nathanian G. Herreshoff. This was a

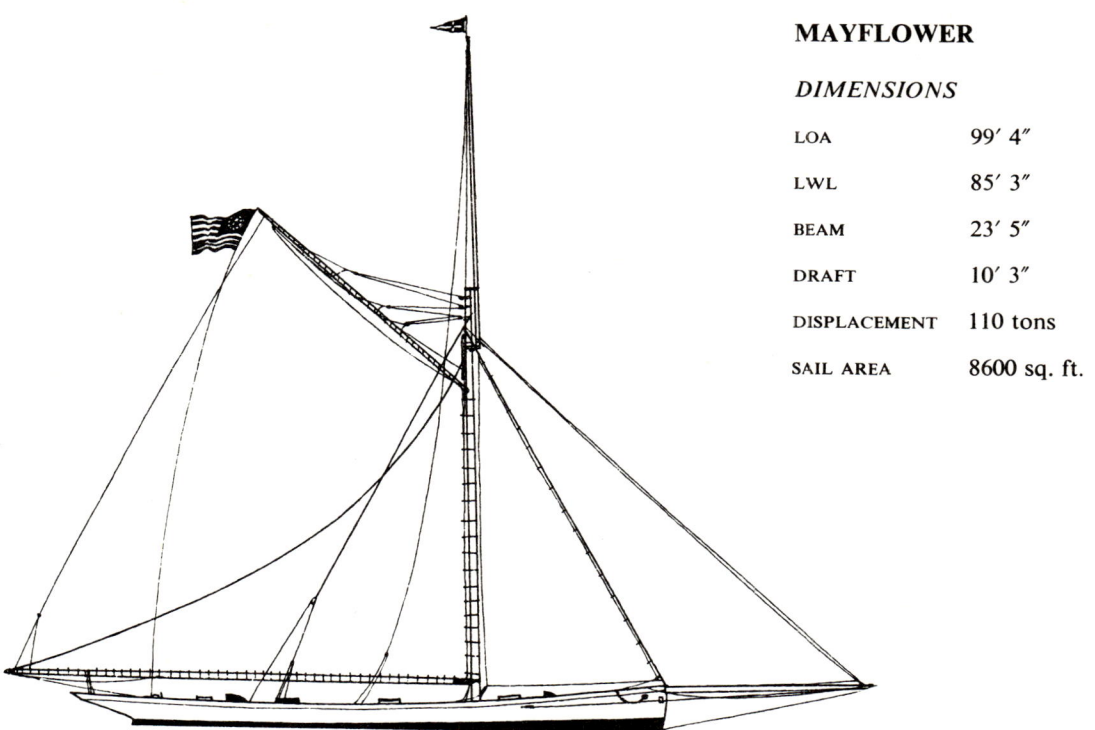

MAYFLOWER

DIMENSIONS

LOA	99′ 4″
LWL	85′ 3″
BEAM	23′ 5″
DRAFT	10′ 3″
DISPLACEMENT	110 tons
SAIL AREA	8600 sq. ft.

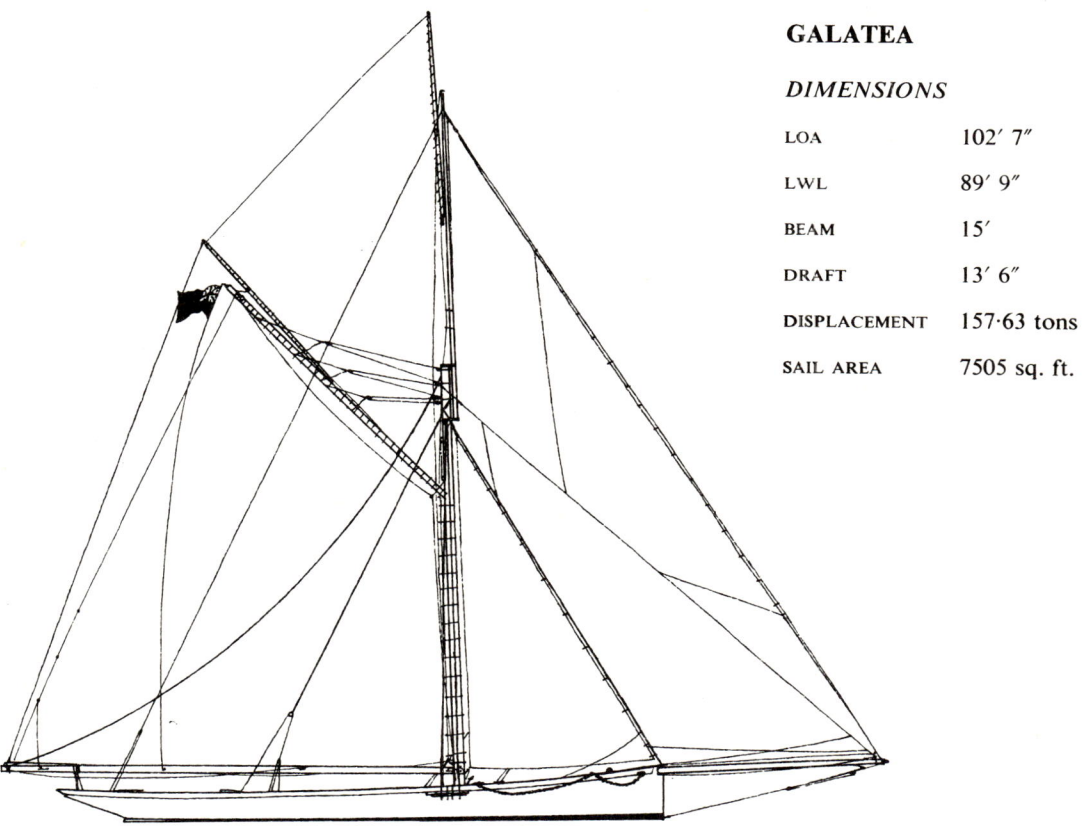

GALATEA

DIMENSIONS

LOA	102′ 7″
LWL	89′ 9″
BEAM	15′
DRAFT	13′ 6″
DISPLACEMENT	157·63 tons
SAIL AREA	7505 sq. ft.

SERIES	DATE	NAME (winners name first)	COURSE	ELAPSED TIME	CORRECTED TIME	WINS BY	REMARKS
6th	September 9 1886	*MAYFLOWER* *GALATEA*	New York Yacht Club Course *2·36 miles*	5.26.41 5.39.21	5.26.41 5.38.43	12m 02s	
6th	September 11 1886	*MAYFLOWER* *GALATEA*	20 miles to leeward from Sandy Hook Lightship and return *40 miles*	6.49.00 7.18.48	6.49.00 7.18.09	29m 09s	

good series, the races interesting and close throughout.

The story is totally different so far as the Earl's second challenge in 1895 is concerned. Once again his yacht was built by G. L. Watson, and the American by Herreshoff and rather appropriately named *Defender*. She was sailed by 'Hank' Haff.

For this series it could be said that Herreshoff turned to British dimensions with a narrower yacht than had been customary in the United States, while G. L. Watson, the Britisher designer, followed the lines of

Vigilant with a much broader-beamed yacht than had been customary on this side of the Atlantic. Both these designers had, so to speak, changed places in this respect. Herreshoff built the first of the real American racing machines. Not only was his introduction of manganese bronze and aluminium for bottom and top plating respectively a completely new development but many thought that the extreme lightness of the American yacht was little short of dangerous. People said her mast would go through the bottom, but in the event she hung together very well. *Valkyrie*

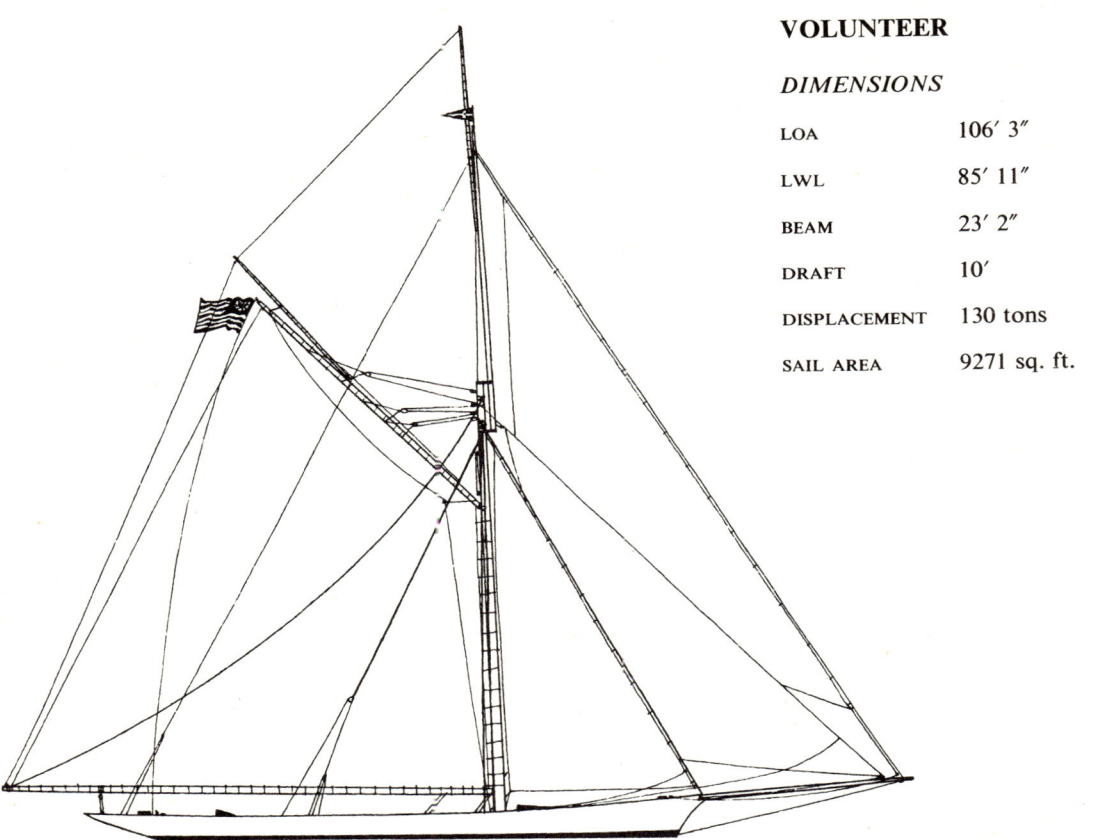

VOLUNTEER

DIMENSIONS

LOA	106′ 3″
LWL	85′ 11″
BEAM	23′ 2″
DRAFT	10′
DISPLACEMENT	130 tons
SAIL AREA	9271 sq. ft.

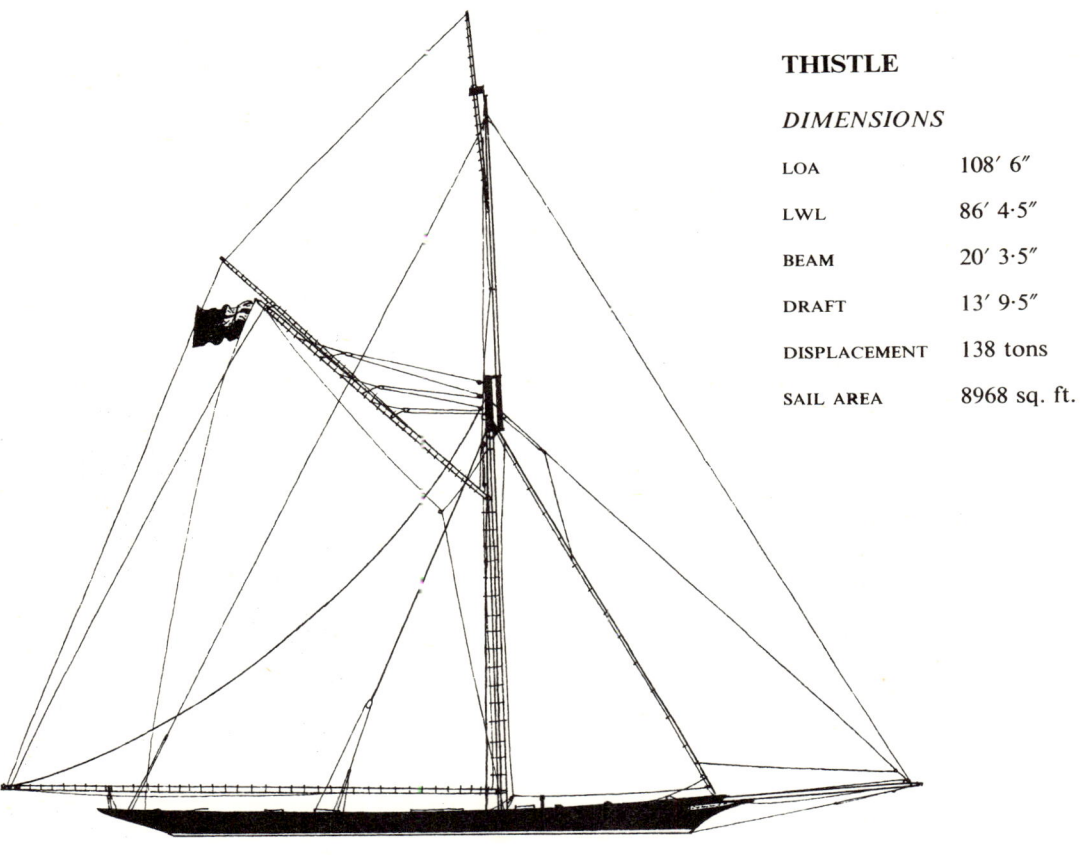

THISTLE

DIMENSIONS

LOA	108′ 6″
LWL	86′ 4·5″
BEAM	20′ 3·5″
DRAFT	13′ 9·5″
DISPLACEMENT	138 tons
SAIL AREA	8968 sq. ft.

SERIES	DATE	NAME (winners name first)	COURSE	ELAPSED TIME	CORRECTED TIME	WINS BY	REMARKS
7th	September 27 1887	*VOLUNTEER* *THISTLE*	New York Yacht Club Course *32·6 miles*	4.53.18 5.12.46·75	4.53.18 5.12.41·75	19m 23·75s	
7th	September 30 1887	*VOLUNTEER* *THISTLE*	20 miles to leeward from Sandy Hook Lightship and return *40 miles*	5.42.56·25 5.54.51	5.42.56·25 5.54.45	11m 48·75s	

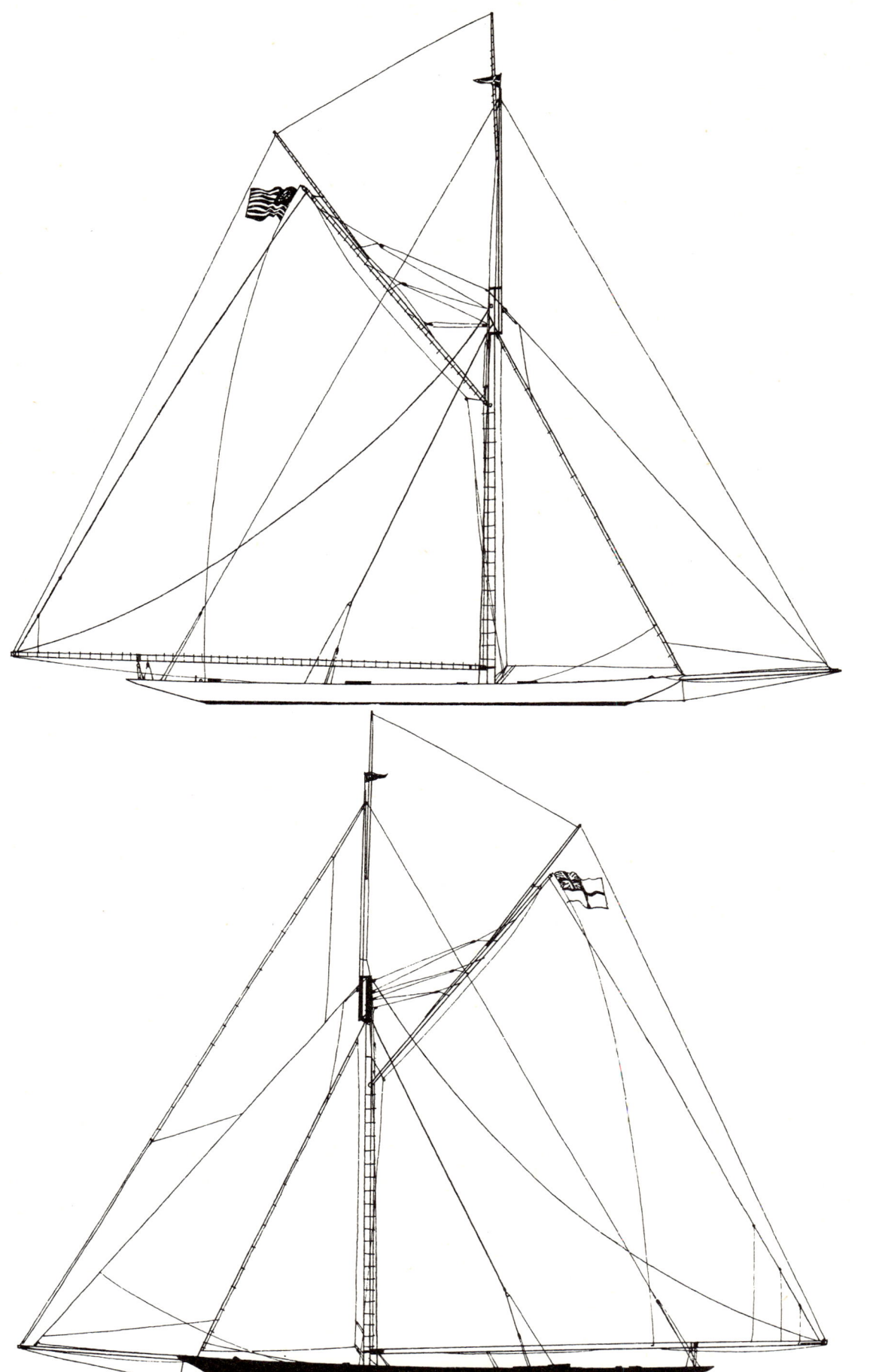

VIGILANT

DIMENSIONS

LOA	128′
LWL	85′ 4″
BEAM	26′
DRAFT	14′ 4″
DISPLACEMENT	96·18 tons
SAIL AREA	11,272 sq. ft.

VALKYRIE II

DIMENSIONS

LOA	133′
LWL	85′ 8″
BEAM	27′ 7″
DRAFT	13′
DISPLACEMENT	93·57 tons
SAIL AREA	10,042 sq. ft.

SERIES	DATE	NAME (winners name first)	COURSE	ELAPSED TIME	CORRECTED TIME	WINS BY	REMARKS
8th	October 7 1893	*VIGILANT* *VALKYRIE II*	15 miles to leeward from Sandy Hook Lightship and return *30 miles*	4.05.47 4.13.23	4.05.47 4.11.35	5m 48s	
8th	October 9 1893	*VIGILANT* *VALKYRIE II*	Equilateral triangle from Sandy Hook Lightship *30 miles*	3.25.01 3.37.24	3.25.01 3.35.36	10m 35s	
8th	October 13 1893	*VIGILANT* *VALKYRIE II*	15 miles to windward from Sandy Hook Lightship and return *30 miles*	3.24.39 3.26.52	3.24.39 3.25.19	0m 40s	

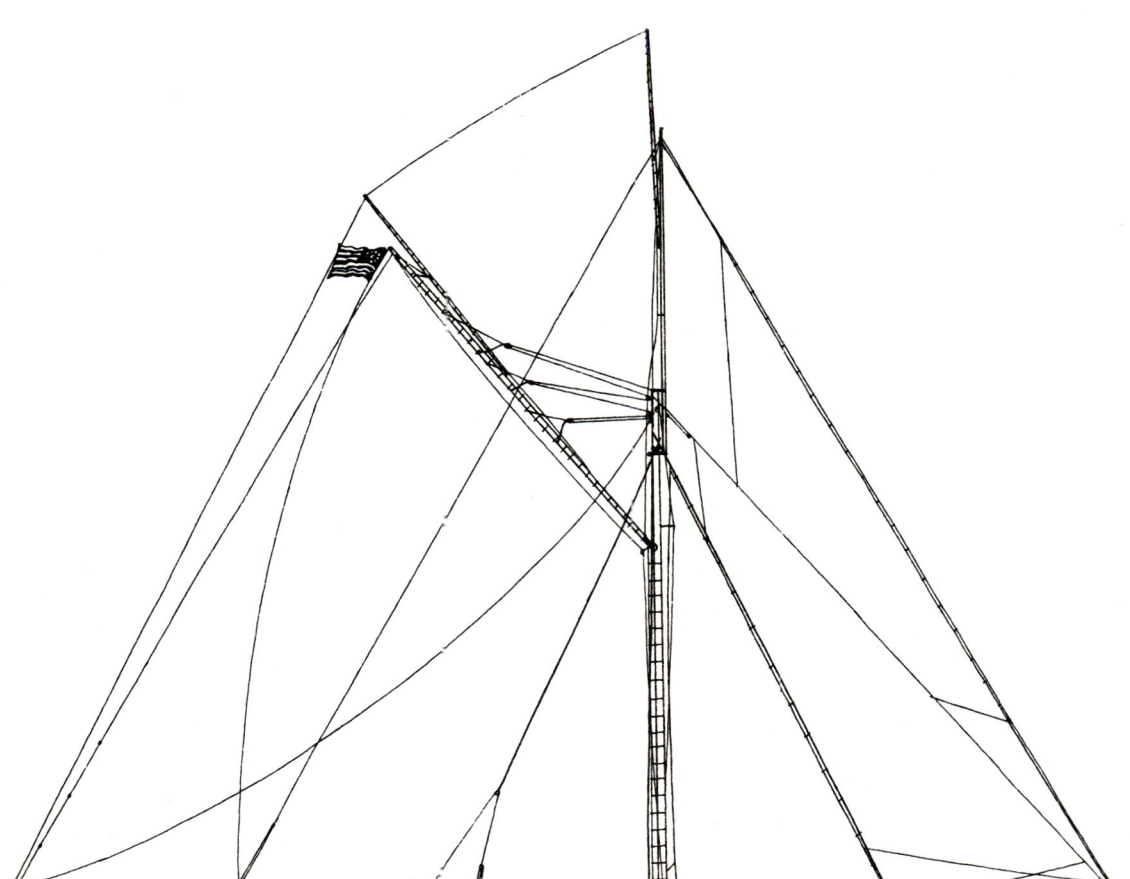

DEFENDER

DIMENSIONS

LOA	124′
LWL	88′ 6″
BEAM	23′ 3″
DRAFT	19′ 6″
DISPLACEMENT	100·36 tons
SAIL AREA	12,602 sq. ft.

SERIES	DATE	NAME (winners name first)	COURSE	ELAPSED TIME	CORRECTED TIME	WINS BY	REMARKS
9th	September 7 1895	*DEFENDER* *VALKYRIE III*	15 miles from mark, 3 miles N.E. of Seabright, New Jersey and return *30 miles*	5.00.24 5.08.44	4.59.55 5.08.44	8m 49s	
9th	September 10 1895	*VALKYRIE III* *DEFENDER*	Equilateral triangle from Sandy Hook Lightship *30 miles*	3.55.09 3.56.25	3.55.09 3.55.56	0m 47s	*VALKYRIE III disqualified for fouling Defender*
9th	September 12 1895	*DEFENDER* *VALKYRIE III*	15 miles to windward from Sandy Hook Lightship and return *30 miles*	4.44.12 DID NOT FINISH	4.43.43		*VALKYRIE III withdrew on crossing the line*

III arrived in America on 18 August 1895 with the doubtful reputation of having sailed races against the Royal Yacht *Britannia*, G. L. Watson's greatest creation, winning one and losing two.

The first race, on 7 September, was nearly cancelled because of the glassy sea, but in the afternoon a light breeze got up and the yachts were sent away for a fifteen-mile straight out and back course, starting at the Scotland light vessel. There was a long swell running, a legacy from earlier bad weather, and this favoured the deep-keel narrow *Defender*, but the lightness of the wind was an advantage to the challenger. This time the yachts did not follow each other with their tacks so the interest lay in seeing how they were placed when they came together when approaching the outer mark. The spectator fleet sensing this had crowded to the mark.

Earlier on, the challenger was seen to be footing faster to windward than *Defender* but the latter had pointed better and cut through the swell so that as the yachts came together after the first long tack they were seen to be almost level. In the event, *Defender* just crossed the bows of the challenger and from that point the challenger never looked like winning. *Defender* rounded the mark well ahead and ran home an easy winner.

Lord Dunraven now made the first of his complaints. He claimed that the *Defender* had more ballast on board after the official measurements had been taken. Both yachts were therefore measured again and the charge was refuted. He also complained that his yacht had been hampered by the spectator fleet.

The second race took place three days later with a triangular course –

each leg being ten miles. All was set for a prompt start at 10.50 when the fleet of excursion steamers began crowding on the yachts. Both yachts were coming down the line close hauled; *Valkyrie*, skippered by Captain Sycamore, was on *Defender*'s weather, waiting to turn and cross, when a big steamer, the *Yorktown*, came right through the line, thus separating the two yachts. As soon as the *Yorktown* was clear it was seen that *Valkyrie* was still on *Defender*'s weather, but had got slightly ahead. With only seconds to go to the start *Valkyrie* swung away slightly across *Defender*'s bow. 'Hank' Haff held his course so that *Valkyrie* had to luff sharply to avoid a collision. In doing so the end of *Valkyrie*'s huge main boom swept right across the deck of the *Defender* and snapped her starboard shroud. It went off like a gun. Immediately her topmast cracked. 'Hank' swung *Defender* up into the wind and Mr Iselin, the official representative of the New York Yacht Club on board, sent up a protest flag. *Valkyrie* meanwhile went hot foot along the first leg of the course. Haff legged it after *Valkyrie* with a temporary shroud rigged, his topsail lowered and his topmast still bending over. Not unexpectedly *Valkyrie* was three minutes ahead on the first leg. On the next leg, which was a reach, 'Hank' risked a topsail and held *Valkyrie* to the second mark. The last leg was a run and *Defender* put up all her light sails and carried them well. She caught up a good deal on the challenger and crossed the line only two minutes eighteen seconds after *Valkyrie* which meant she lost by a mere 45 seconds on corrected time.

The New York Yacht Club had been set a tricky problem which they

DIMENSIONS

LOA	126'
LWL	89' 9"
BEAM	26' 2"
DRAFT	19' 7"
DISPLACEMENT	101·47 tons
SAIL AREA	13,028 sq. ft.

tried to solve by arranging for a resail by mutual consent, but the idea never got them anywhere so they collected all the evidence and photographs and formally disqualified *Valkyrie*. The rule they quoted says that a yacht must not bear away to prevent a yacht from passing her to leeward. Mr Iselin immediately offered to sail the race again, but Lord Dunraven declined in a strongly worded letter. The personal situation was now tense and made worse by further letter-writing in which Lord Dunraven again complained of the crowding by the spectator fleet.

On the evening of the 11th, the Committee of the New York Yacht Club met to consider the vexed situation with regard to the spectator fleet. They were assisted in this particular matter by the press which headlined the nuisance, so that when the yachts made ready to race on the 12th, the fleet of excursion boats and private yachts left all the water that could be desired for a fair start. *Defender* appeared with a new topmast and set a full rig, but it was clear to all present that something strange was afoot with *Valkyrie*. She appeared to be in perfect trim but had not bothered to set her full quota of sails, although conditions called for this. When the starting gun was fired she crossed the line and immediately recrossed it and returned to harbour. *Defender* sailed alone over the course and was declared the winner. The America's Cup and all it meant in international yacht racing and sportsmanship had sunk to its lowest ebb.

It would take a major part in a book to tell the full story of the Dunraven Affair. Articles appeared in national papers in many countries. Those in the United States supported the New York Yacht Club and those

in England did not show any liking for the conduct of the Earl. Some said this could be the end of the America's Cup and British yachtsmen kept very low, apparently having lost all interest. Suffice it to say that when Captain Sycamore bore away to lose a second or two so that he would not reach the end of the starting line before the gun fired, he may not have appreciated that as he luffed up to cross the line his long boom could sweep the deck of *Defender* if 'Hank' Haff held his course, which he had the right to do. Furthermore, it is true that while *Defender* was lying alongside her tender, the *Hattie Palmer*, some ballast was shifted during the night. The reason for this was that, since *Valkyrie III* did not have bulkheads and interior fittings on board, *Defender* was at liberty to remove hers and replace them with ballast as an alternative. This entailed sixty-three pigs of lead being stored and as some of these did not fit in very well they were taken on board the *Hattie Palmer* for reshaping.

If the America's Cup was to be revised and its purpose as stated in the two Deeds of Gift brought to fruition, someone had to come forward whose ideals and sportsmanship fitted the situation. There were rumours of challengers during the next few years including one from Australia, but nothing came of them, and then, out of the blue, a challenge came from a most unexpected quarter and on behalf of a most improbable person.

In the late summer of 1895 the Royal Ulster Yacht Club of Belfast, Northern Ireland, challenged on behalf of one of its members, a tea merchant by the name of Thomas Lipton.

CHAPTER 4

The *Shamrock* Story

The Lipton challenges are a story in themselves and constitute an era in the America's Cup races which served to place the contests on the high level of skill, design and sportsmanship which the Deed of Gift commanded.

The first of these challenges was significant in that the defender and challenger were built as 'racing machines' solely for the purpose of these races. Measurement rules were closely studied and everything possible vas done to take the slightest advantage of any loophole. At this time the governing rule was based on length of waterline when upright and on an even keel. Consequently underbodies were cut away and ends were lengthened out, which gave a short length on handicap and a long length when racing and heeled over. Keels were thin with a massive lump of lead at the bottom weighing anything up to 80 or 90 tons. But apart from the yachts themselves, by the turn of the century a factor had come on the scene which also profoundly influenced affairs. This was expense. Very few individual people were able to finance a challenge or build a defender, and the contest in 1899 set a pattern which was to run for the next half century in that only one nation, Great Britain, continued to challenge.

Lipton went to William Fife, whose terms of reference were to turn out the fastest boat which money could provide. The yacht was built by Thorneycroft, well known as experts in light ship construction. Her mast, boom and gaff were all made of light steel, which was wont to buckle, thus disturbing the set of the sails. Nevertheless, this yacht was judged a dangerous competitor and on trials she was known to have travelled at over 13 knots on a reach. The challenge coming from Ireland, she was named *Shamrock*.

After some rather inconclusive races against the well-known royal racer *Britannia*, *Shamrock* left England on 3 August 1899 to sail to New York 'on her own bottom' as the Deed stipulated. Her particulars (given in full here to compare with the defender) were:

LENGTH OVERALL   129 feet

LENGTH WATERLINE   89 feet 8 inches

BEAM   25 feet

DRAUGHT   20 feet 3 inches

SAIL AREA   13,492 square feet.

Her bottom plating was manganese bronze. Above water she was aluminium. At the foot of her deep keel she carried over 70 tons of lead.

Before reaching New York Tommy Lipton obtained permission to tow his challenger some of the way using his steam yacht *Erin*. This permission, to tow when expedient, was another concession by the New York Yacht Club and gladly given. All the same, some responsible opinion was voiced against the advisability of towing a yacht of so light a construction as this could be asking for trouble with planks 'starting' and rivets pulling, but *Shamrock* arrived in New York in good shape and was much admired.

No individual in the New York Yacht Club could find the money to build a defender alone. So a syndicate was formed, headed by J. Pierpont Morgan, with C. Oliver Iselin, a yachtsman of vast experience in large boats, as manager. Herreshoff, as one might have expected, was appointed designer and builder. Secrecy was now introduced into this business and no information leaked out to the public until the yacht appeared complete and ready for racing. She was named *Columbia*. Surprisingly her particulars compared closely with *Shamrock*'s:

LENGTH OVERALL	131 feet
LENGTH WATERLINE	89 feet 8 inches
BEAM	24 feet
DRAUGHT	19 feet 3 inches
SAIL AREA	13,135 square feet.

Her bottom plating was manganese bronze. Above water she was sheathed with steel. At the foot of her 19-foot fin keel she carried 90 tons of lead.

While both yachts were similar in many material particulars, there were marked differences in their skippers. The Americans picked a man named Charles Barr. This selection raised some eyebrows more than a little as Barr was until recently a Scot and the ink on his United States naturalisation papers was hardly dry. But if ever a wise choice was made this was it. Charlie Barr stands out for all time as probably the ablest skipper who ever sailed in these contests. There was, too, on the American side, another helpful factor. *Defender* was commissioned to tune up *Columbia* and until three races had been sailed the eventual defender was not named. This was a great test between two superb yachts. Both were worthy of the honour to defend but racing depends on so many factors which can tip the scales and this time it was the skipper. Charlie Barr established a clear superiority over *Defender*'s skipper and *Columbia* was named to defend the Cup.

Shamrock had a very good skipper too in Archie Hogarth, a proven first class professional, but if a man is not born with the gift of inspired helmsmanship he surely cannot acquire it. Also on the English side they had to face a stroke of bad luck. Just before the first race was due to be sailed, William Fife was taken ill and although *Shamrock* carried some experienced and talented yachtsmen Fife, as the man who had built the boat and perhaps the most knowledgeable of all in the team, could have brought just those fine points of advice to the challenger which might have off-set in part, at least, Charlie Barr's uncanny touch and judgement.

The first race was a straight leg, fifteen miles to windward and back, from the Sandy Hook light vessel, and on 2 October both yachts came up to the starting line in excellent shape. The vast size of the excursion fleet would have sent Lord Dunraven back to harbour without making a contest, but the government of the United States had taken a hand this time and had provided an opposing fleet of revenue cutters and torpedo boats, so that the starting line at least was kept clear. The size of the spectator fleet was a reflection of the opinion that it was going to be a closely matched race under the fairest conditions so far arranged for the Cup between yachts remarkably similar.

The starting gun boomed at 11.15 and *Shamrock* crossed the line 43 seconds ahead of *Columbia*. This was what so many people had come to see and excitement was immense. Indeed the day could have been one of drama, but this was foiled by the wind which died away.

Before reaching the outer mark *Columbia* got a lucky favourable puff and overtook *Shamrock*, later rounding the mark two minutes ahead, but with conditions changing every quarter of an hour *Shamrock* had her share of the luck and shortly drew level. Then to the great disappointment of all concerned, the wind died away completely and it was clear that neither yacht could finish in the time allowance of five and a half hours.

Unfortunately these conditions prevailed for nearly a fortnight with one race after another having to be abandoned and crews feeling the strain more and more.

It was therefore with everyone rather on edge that both yachts came out to the now famous lightship on 16 October. At least the wind was fresh but some fog persisted and an ocean tug was detailed to go ahead and point the way to the outer mark. *Columbia* got slightly the better of the start and the rather steep seas on the beat out seemed to trouble *Shamrock* rather more than *Columbia*. Charlie Barr was able therefore to keep *Shamrock* on his lee quarter all the way and rounded some nine minutes ahead. *Shamrock* had no hope of catching *Columbia* on the run home and Barr crossed the finishing line over 10 minutes ahead.

The next day conditions were similar except that the fog had all but gone. This time the course was triangular, of which the first leg was a beat. The start was full of good tacking and reaching which delighted the spectators and when the starting gun was fired *Shamrock* raced over the line two seconds in the lead, but *Columbia* was to windward. This time *Columbia* did not manage to draw away and both yachts, with everything up and close hauled, drove their way neck and neck to windward for some twenty-five minutes, truly a magnificent sight; but experienced yachtsmen were doubtful whether this could be kept up with masts pared for weight holding up massive sail areas. Something had to give way in one of the yachts. Sadly it was *Shamrock* which took the knock. Suddenly her huge topsail collapsed, the topmast having snapped clean off close to the mainmast head.

Hogarth immediately went into the wind and the crew swarmed aloft to clear the mess, but *Shamrock* was out of the race and *Columbia* sailed over.

In the circumstances it might have been supposed that the defender would offer to sail the race again, as had been done in previous races, notably by Sir John Sutton in his challenger when the defender's gear failed. In this case, however, it was not possible because one of the clauses in the mutual agreement in this series was that if a yacht came by any accident then there would be no re-race. This stipulation did have the effect of putting some brake on the phenomenally light construction of masts and spars allied to vast areas of canvas.

The contest had now been in operation for eighteen days, so with fog and the disaster to *Shamrock* the spectator fleet had, by and large, given up coming out. Consequently on 20 October the start was free of any obstructions and this was just as well because there was a brisk northerly wind and some small breakers, in fact a spanking day for the straight course once again. In these conditions *Shamrock* was carrying only a small storm topsail and *Columbia*, playing really safe, hoisted no topsail at all. This was a day when *Shamrock* could show to advantage and she started well enough by leading *Columbia* over the line by one minute.

COLUMBIA

DIMENSIONS

LOA	132'
LWL	90'
BEAM	24' 2"
DRAFT	19' 10"
DISPLACEMENT	102·13 tons
SAIL AREA	13,135 sq. ft.

SHAMROCK I

DIMENSIONS

LOA	129' 9"
LWL	89'
BEAM	24' 6"
DRAFT	20' 2"
DISPLACEMENT	102·56 tons
SAIL AREA	13,492 sq. ft.

SERIES	DATE	NAME (winners name first)	COURSE	ELAPSED TIME	CORRECTED TIME	WINS BY	REMARKS
10th	October 16 1899	*COLUMBIA* *SHAMROCK*	15 miles to windward from Sandy Hook Lightship and return *30 miles*	4.53.53 5.04.07	4.53.53 5.04.01	10m s	
10th	October 17 1899	*COLUMBIA* *SHAMROCK*	Equilateral triangle from Sandy Hook Lightship *30 miles*	3.37.00 DID NOT FINISH	3.37.00		*SHAMROCK carried away top mast and withdrew*
10th	October 20 1899	*COLUMBIA* *SHAMROCK*	15 miles to windward from Sandy Hook Lightship and return *30 miles*	3.38.25 3.44.43	3.38.09 3.44.43	6m 34s	

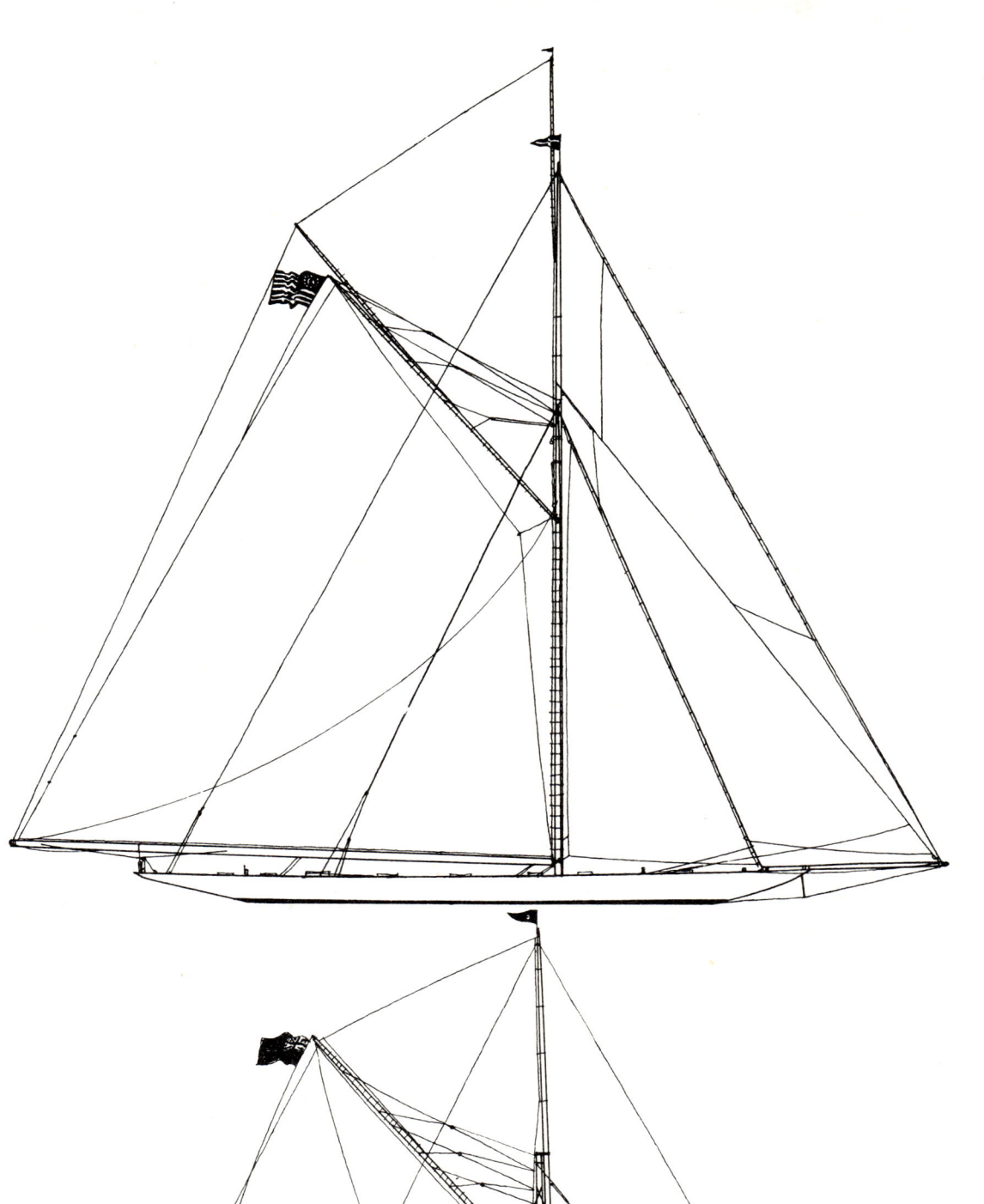

COLUMBIA

DIMENSIONS

LOA	132′
LWL	90′
BEAM	24′ 2″
DRAFT	19′ 10″
DISPLACEMENT	102·13 tons
SAIL AREA	13,135 sq. ft.

SHAMROCK II

DIMENSIONS

LOA	134′ 6″
LWL	90′
BEAM	24′ 2″
DRAFT	20′ 10″
DISPLACEMENT	128·77 tons
SAIL AREA	14,027 sq. ft.

SERIES	DATE	NAME (winners name first)	COURSE	ELAPSED TIME	CORRECTED TIME	WINS BY	REMARKS
11th	September 28 1901	*COLUMBIA* *SHAMROCK II*	15 miles to windward from Sandy Hook Lightship and return *30 miles*	4.31.07 4.31.44	4.30.24 4.31.44	1m 24s	
11th	October 3 1901	*COLUMBIA* *SHAMROCK II*	Equilateral triangle from Sandy Hook Lightship *30 miles*	3.13.18 3.16.10	3.12.35 3.16.10	3m 35s	
11th	October 4 1901	*COLUMBIA* *SHAMROCK II*	15 miles to leeward from Sandy Hook Lightship and return *30 miles*	4.33.40 4.33.38	4.32.57 4.33.38	0m 41s	

The leg out to the mark was a run and Charlie Barr dared his big spinnaker. *Shamrock* meanwhile, still smarting from her broken topmast, hoisted only a medium-sized sail. But this was sound tactics too as *Columbia*'s crew struggled to get their mighty balloon to draw fully. Eventually, having parted one spinnaker boom in the process, they did get the big sail set and *Columbia* began to draw up on *Shamrock*. Not content with this progress Barr hoisted his topsail, bringing heart throbs to all spectators still with the yachts, but the masts held out and *Columbia* rounded the mark just ahead of *Shamrock* – a bit lucky perhaps, but when you are astern you must do something if you are to win the race. As soon as he was round the mark, Barr housed both spinnaker and topsail and settled down to the beat back, just seventeen seconds ahead of *Shamrock*, with the mainsail and two jibs flat aft and drawing beautifully.

For the same reason that Barr took risks on the run it was *Shamrock*'s turn now to pile on the canvas, but this was not the real answer on a beat and rightly Hogarth 'sailed' his yacht with the correct amount of canvas for the conditions, and tried first bearing away and then pinching up to see if he could bridge that small gap. Charlie Barr kept steadily on never altering his course, his sails, or the trim of his yacht. With only a few miles to go and still astern, Hogarth rightly risked his topsail – he put up a big one. This time the topmast held but the effect was only to heel the yacht over more, so *Columbia* crossed the line the winner by six minutes.

The first of the *Shamrock* series was over and the critics of Barr had to eat their words. Both yachts were first class of their type, both crews were very good, but in Barr the Americans had picked a brilliant helmsman. Yet people wondered whether things might have been different if Fife had been able to be in *Shamrock*'s after-guard. Who knows?

It seemed clear to all English yachtsmen that, judging from the *Shamrock I* series, we could do better and probably win. So also thought Lipton, whose next challenge brought about 'the closest ever' to date. Indeed no story of the America's Cup can pass over the *Shamrock II* series, regardless of the just claims of other contests and other yachts on the basis of their contribution to yachting and yacht building.

Tommy Lipton, through the Royal Ulster Yacht Club, challenged in 1900 asking for races in 1901. This was immediately accepted by the New York Yacht Club. Lipton this time went to G. L. Watson for *Shamrock II*. This great designer, who made his reputation with the King's yacht *Britannia*, had also built the *Valkyries* and *Thistle*, the Scottish challenger. Watson added to his reputation by conducting the first tank tests on experimental models, so far as yachts were concerned.

On the other side of the Atlantic the now almost standard procedure was carried out, in that the New York Yacht Club formed a syndicate and built a yacht specially for the defence of the Cup. Herreshoff as ever was the builder, and the yacht was called *Constitution*.

Two events altered the even tenor of this customary procedure. Firstly Charlie Barr in *Columbia* beat *Constitution* in the eliminating trials and *Columbia* was selected to defend. Herreshoff was quite astonished when his new boat was beaten by his older one but then, as people said, what do helmsmen do against Barr? There was also a moment of tension when the Boston Yacht Club produced a yacht and stated that they wished to 'come

in' on this matter of the defence of the Cup. Mr Lawson, owner of the Boston yacht *Independence*, accordingly found himself matched against both Herreshoff yachts and was soundly beaten by both. Had he won he could only have represented America by becoming a member of the New York Yacht Club and this, he had already stated, he had no intention of doing. Fortunately, what might have been a serious clash between the two yacht clubs and between great yachtsmen was averted gracefully and very fairly by Herreshoff and Charlie Barr.

So *Shamrock II* sailed against the same defender designed and skippered by these two champions of their arts. The challenger differed little from *Shamrock I* except that she carried an even larger spread of sail – 14,290 square feet as compared with 13,135 – and, provided everything held together, she certainly had a chance to lift the Cup. The races were staggeringly close. In the first, *Columbia* won by 1 minute 20 seconds, in the second by 3 minutes 35 seconds and in the third by 41 seconds. This last and final race was fantastic. The course was the usual fifteen miles out and back, the return trip being the beat. As the yachts came towards the finishing line they were almost alongside each other and amid the wildest of excitement *Shamrock* crossed 2 seconds ahead of *Columbia* but had to allow the defender 43 seconds and thus lost by 41 seconds. This has remained the closest finish in the history of the Cup.

In analysis, it was shown that after 90 miles of sailing – and this does not count the distances travelled when tacking – *Columbia* beat *Shamrock* by a total of 3 minutes and 27 seconds actual sailing time. The men who did this feat against Barr were Captains Sycamore and Wringe, the former the helmsman of *Valkyrie III* and the latter number two to Archie Hogarth in *Shamrock I*.

CHAPTER 5

Reliance — the *Shamrock* Story Continued

Reliance earns a place in this book because she was the ultimate example of the 'skimming dish'. Her hull was as flat as could be and she was kept upright by a massive weight of lead at the foot of a 20-foot keel. Herreshoff gave her the largest sail area ever provided in the history of the Cup. It was 16,160 square feet.

Lipton went back to Fife for *Shamrock III* and, although the design was more balanced than that of the defender, the sail area was vast. This was carried on a hull reminiscent of the narrow cutter type.

The particulars of these two yachts show only 2 foot 8 inch differences in beam but this is a good deal when viewing the hull as a whole. Although quoted elsewhere, the particulars of these two yachts are especially interesting:

Reliance

LENGTH OVERALL	143 feet 8 inches
LENGTH WATERLINE	89 feet 8 inches
BEAM	25 feet 8 inches
DRAUGHT	20 feet
SAIL AREA	16,160 square feet (3000 square feet more than

Columbia).

The forward overhang was 28 feet and the after overhang 26 feet. When heeled over she increased her bearing surface from 90 feet to 130 feet. The hull was very flat – the ultimate 'skimming dish'.

Shamrock

LENGTH OVERALL	134 feet 4 inches
LENGTH WATERLINE	89 feet 10 inches
BEAM	23 feet
DRAUGHT	19 feet
SAIL AREA	14,145 square feet.

This yacht was only 8 inches wider than *Valkyrie II*, one of the 'plank on edge' types. She was constructed of nickel steel coated with white enamel. Besides being a swing back to the narrow cutter type she was the first English yacht to be steered by a wheel.

It was not long before *Reliance* was in trouble. She lost her mast in one working-up race, but without disastrous results, and sometimes failed to turn up for an important preliminary race because she was in dock. In fact the writing was on the wall for these unseamanlike racing machines, particularly since the news from England was not much better. *Shamrock III* also lost a mast when sailing against *Shamrock I* in Weymouth Bay, when she was hit by a sudden squall. A man was drowned in the confusion which followed, an incident which shocked Tommy Lipton more than anything else in his quest for the Cup.

The result of all this was that the New York Yacht Club brought in a temporary rule, that if the Committee thought the wind too strong for these vast areas of sail on lightly constructed boats, they had the power to cancel the race. This ruling brought the America's Cup racing to a point so far removed from the ideas of the Deed of Gift• being done in research or on the drawing board which would further yachting as a whole.

On 20 August 1903 the morning was calm and both boats were ready at the usual starting place, namely the Sandy Hook light vessel. Captain Wringe sailing *Shamrock* made a good start beating *Reliance* to the line, but there seemed to be something uncanny about the American yacht under the touch of Charlie Barr at the helm.

With his immense sail area he had to allow *Shamrock* 1 minute 57 seconds over a 30 mile course, but *Reliance* under handicap never seemed to weigh heavily on the shoulders of the American syndicate. The race was the customary 15 miles out and back and, as the day went on, the wind steadily fell until it was clear that the time limit would be overrun. When the Committee called it off *Reliance* was far ahead of *Shamrock III* as everyone had expected she would be in light airs.

Two days later the yachts were again at the starting point. It was 52 years to the day that the *America* had gone round the Isle of Wight leaving all British contenders miles behind. This time the breeze was good and there was a choppy sea. *Reliance* built like a tea-tray did not like these conditions while *Shamrock*, with her cutter type hull, slipped through the sea without fuss. Barr stood in shore to get the calmer water and sailing at great speed tacked out to the mark. Both yachts came to the buoy on level terms. At this point the British crew made an error which cost them the race, by sending up the spinnaker with a turn in it. By the time they had got it down and up again Barr had taken *Reliance* so far ahead that the result was never in doubt.

The next race was on the 25th, a weekend having intervened. As usual the second race was a triangular course, the first leg of which was a beat, which *Reliance* won by 2 minutes 37 seconds, but on corrected time and allowing for the failure of *Shamrock* to make a good start, it showed that *Reliance* had reached the first mark in 54 seconds less time than the challenger.

The next leg was a straightforward reach and here again Barr did the better. As it was possible at one point to carry spinnakers, *Shamrock* hoped that their spinnaker drill might this time show to their advantage, but the crew of *Reliance* were too well trained and making no mistakes gained another 1 minute 20 seconds.

For the last leg the wind had slightly changed and instead of a run it was a reach, rather similar to the second leg. *Reliance* again tried her spinnaker but could not get it to draw well while *Shamrock* made no attempt at this exercise at all. With both yachts grasping at every slight shift of the wind, the race was nearly over when *Reliance* ran into a patch of almost complete calm. *Shamrock* came bowling along until both yachts were close together, but then it was *Shamrock*'s turn to be almost becalmed and *Reliance* made the best of her clear superiority in very light winds and crossed the finishing line a winner by 1 minute 19 seconds on corrected time.

Now came nine days of utter frustration when both yachts failed to finish a course. First it was no wind and then, to the horror of all deepsea yachtsmen, on a day of strong winds, the Committee invoked the special rule and called off the race. On another day there was dense fog.

The final race was sailed on 3 September and most people agreed at the conclusion that it was really best forgotten. Once again in the light airs Barr had sailed *Reliance* to perfection and brought her to the first mark

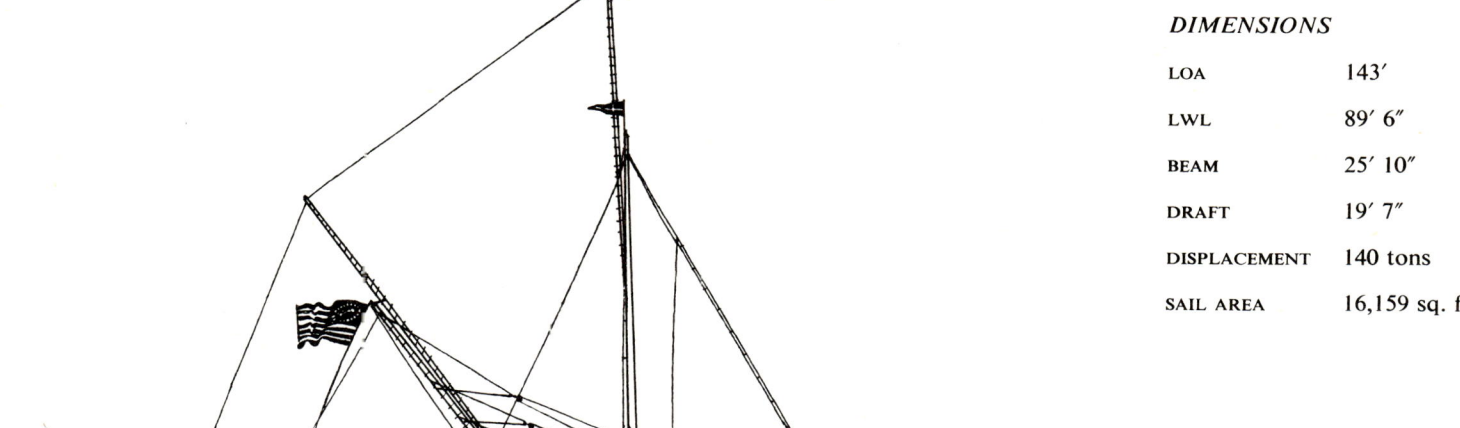

RELIANCE

DIMENSIONS

LOA	143'
LWL	89' 6"
BEAM	25' 10"
DRAFT	19' 7"
DISPLACEMENT	140 tons
SAIL AREA	16,159 sq. ft.

SERIES	DATE	NAME (winners name first)	COURSE	ELAPSED TIME	CORRECTED TIME	WINS BY	REMARKS
12th	August 22 1903	*RELIANCE* *SHAMROCK III*	15 miles to windward from Sandy Hook Lightship and return *30 miles*	3.32.17 3.41.17	3.32.17 3.39.20	7m 03s	.
12th	August 25 1903	*RELIANCE* *SHAMROCK III*	Equilateral triangle from Sandy Hook Lightship *30 miles*	3.14.54 3.18.10	3.14.54 3.16.12	1m 19s	
12th	September 3 1903	*RELIANCE* *SHAMROCK III*	15 miles to windward from Sandy Hook Lightship and return *30 miles*	4.28.06 DID NOT FINISH	4.28.06		

over 11 minutes ahead of the challenger. The superiority was devastating. *Shamrock*'s crew did all they could and showed up particularly well at the turn getting their spinnaker set in remarkably quick time, so much so that it seemed there might be a chance of catching up a bit as it was drawing very well. Then at this point, fog came down. Now there was less interest in the race than in what might become of the yachts. The air was filled with sounds of fog horns, sirens, whistles and the low growl of the Sandy Hook light vessel adding gloom to the whole proceedings.

Barr now exercised his local knowledge. After what seemed to be an interminable time he suddenly appeared out of the gloom and crossed the line close to the Committee boat and within the time limit. To those present this seemed almost incidental to the anxiety over *Shamrock* until, as suddenly as it came down the fog lifted, to reveal *Shamrock* a long way

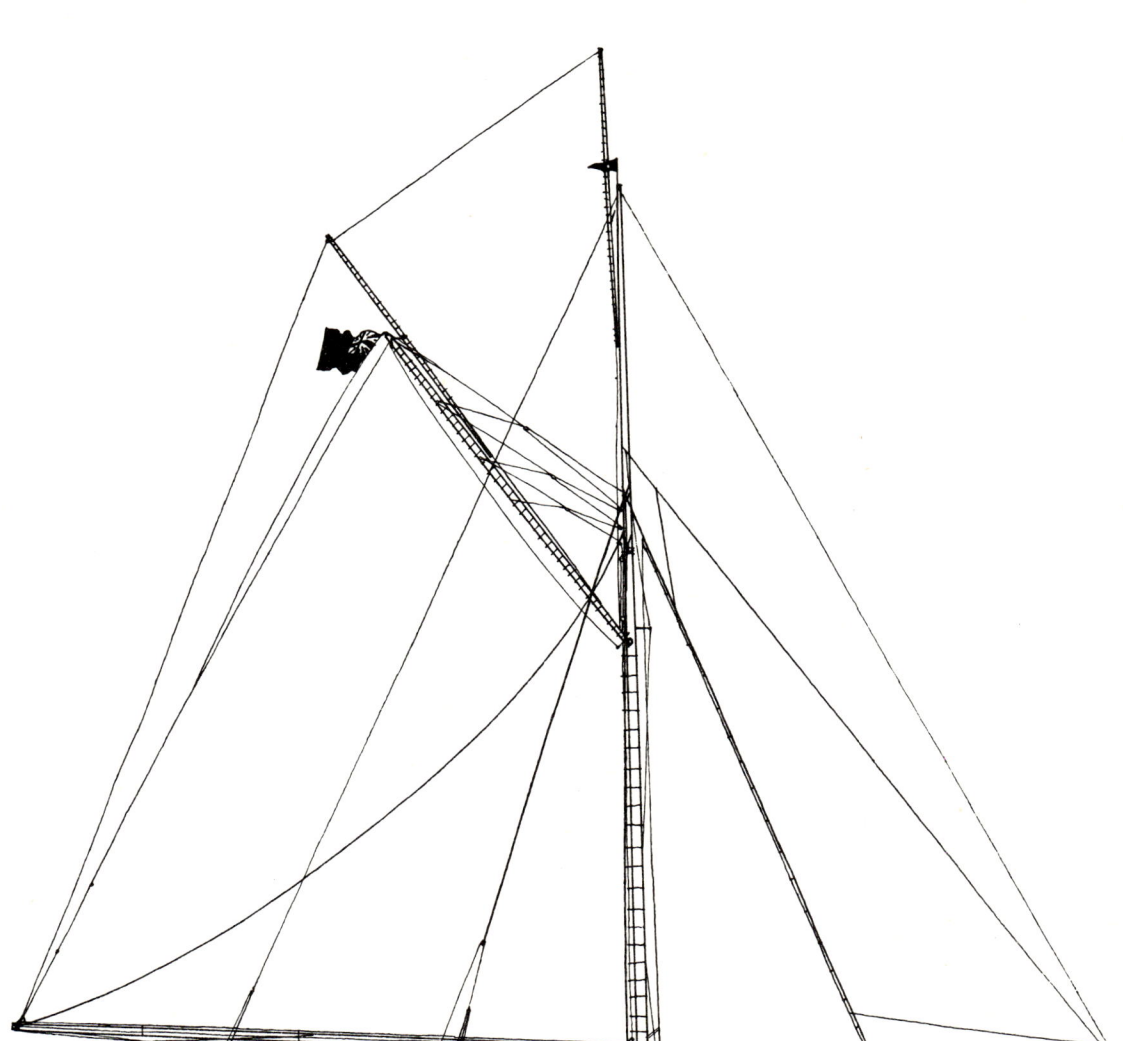

DIMENSIONS

LOA	135'
LWL	90'
BEAM	23' 6"
DRAFT	19' 8"
DISPLACEMENT	138·94 tons
SAIL AREA	14,154 sq. ft.

off course and miles behind.

The series was now over with *Reliance*, the ultimate of racing machines, in the hands of a brilliant helmsman, an easy winner in three straight races. It was a sad time for the indomitable Tommy Lipton. He had taken immense trouble in bringing out *Shamrock I* as a pace-setter for number *III*. This was a very good move and when his minor fleet of steam yachts and two racing yachts arrived in New York harbour they made a great impression and every one had looked forward to even closer racing than with *Shamrock II*. His *Shamrock III* had not done so well as *Shamrock II* in 1901 and at no time in all the racing had *Shamrock III* been leading at any mark. Public opinion summed it up with the conclusion that it was useless to try and 'lift the old mug', as Lipton used to say, and indeed the America's Cup was destined to be forgotten for a decade.

CHAPTER 6

Resolute — the *Shamrock* Story Concluded

The pause in challenging and defending, covering a whole decade, gave yacht clubs time to think and on both sides of the Atlantic rules were put forward with the object of preventing the recurrence of any more *Reliances*. Everyone yearned for seaworthy yet fast yachts, which could sail safely round the world and contribute to the advance of international yacht racing.

With these considerations in view and knowing that he had the wholehearted support of all true yachtsmen, Sir Thomas Lipton sent a challenge in 1913 through the Royal Ulster Yacht Club. At the suggestion of the Club and on his behalf, the New York Yacht Club was asked to name a yacht of not more than 75 feet waterline length. But the Club could not accept this, as the Deed of Gift still stipulated that the challenge must be unconditional. Lipton considered this for some time and then, on the advice of his club, sent an unconditional challenge. The New York Yacht Club immediately accepted this and replied saying that the defender would be 75 feet waterline length. So the terms of the Deed were upheld and Sir Thomas's wish met.

The Americans went to work on this challenge with enthusiasm and in their usual manner. No less than three defenders were built, two for separate syndicates of the New York Yacht Club and one for a private owner. Herreshoff was still on the scene and his yacht, built for one of the syndicates, was named *Resolute*.

Trials were carried out in the summer of 1914 and yet again Herreshoff's design, this time with a 75-foot waterline, did rather better than the other two, but this was not altogether a popular win because in spite of all that had been said in the last decade his yacht was built of the lightest construction. Although she won a high percentage of the trial races, like *Reliance* in 1903 she was repeatedly in dock for repairs and annoyed the others by sometimes not turning up for the races at all.

On the British side *Shamrock IV*, the product of C. E. Nicholson of Gosport, the most successful yacht designer of that time in England, was half-way across the Atlantic when war was declared. She carried on to America but by mutual consent the series was postponed indefinitely.

After such a world-shattering event as the First World War, when peace came in 1918 at first there was only talk as far as the America's Cup was concerned. Yet the challenge was something of a fascination to Englishmen, not least to Sir Thomas Lipton, and in 1920 he renewed his challenge with *Shamrock IV*. Basic terms were quickly agreed, that races should be held every other week-day until one yacht had won three. One point, however, nearly brought a change. The New York Yacht Club suggested a course off Newport, Rhode Island, pointing out that the winds were better there and it would be difficult for the massive spectator fleet to come all that way while real yachtsmen would manage to do so. Sir Thomas, admittedly a bit of a showman, disagreed and so the Americans settled for the old course off the Sandy Hook light vessel.

The same two yachts which would have sailed in the summer of 1914 came out to begin the post-war matches. *Resolute* was a bit lucky to be there. She was skippered by Charlie Adams, an amateur, who had had to work very hard against a new yacht, the *Vanitee*, skippered by George Nichols and C. Sherman Hoyt, the latter particularly brilliant and of whom more will be heard later.

Shamrock IV was in the hands of William Burton, himself a brilliant amateur skipper. As Adams was also an amateur this was the first time in the history of the Cup that two amateurs sailed against each other.

The first race, on 15 July, was full of incident. At the start Burton misjudged, and his sails were not full when the starting gun was fired. Next he sailed too far off the wind and, although going fast, his rival *Resolute* did better by laying the mark and keeping steadily on a set course towards it. At this point a thunderstorm struck the yachts and the wind shifted all over the place. *Resolute* got the better of the guess work and was half a mile ahead with the outer mark not far distant. Burton countered by tacking close in-shore to look for a better wind but never found it and lost almost another half mile. *Resolute* seemed set to round the mark with a clear lead, and as the rest of the course would be 'all downhill' the result looked like a win for the defender, when suddenly her mainsail came hurtling down and about half of it lay over the side. She was only a quarter of a mile from the mark so rounded it with the mainsail only half hoisted and then lowered it altogether sailing on her jib only. It was the storm which had brought this disaster. The rain had soaked the mainsail so that it had shrunk, putting a tremendous strain on the throat halyards and these had parted.

Shamrock now took things steadily and sailed over the course looking really good and going very fast. As she crossed the finishing line another storm burst but Burton kept all his sail up and the gear stood the test very well. *Resolute* gave up and did not finish the course, making her the only defender in the history of the Cup to retire during a race. Adams was severely criticised for this, particularly since the leg home was a run and he might have set his spinnaker and made quite a race of it after all.

A fluky wind prevented any further racing until 20 July when the wind was again light, but the Committee decided to set the yachts off on a triangular course. *Shamrock* did not start well. The first leg was a very broad reach and Burton tried a large balloon jib. This had been stopped up and hoisted before the start and when it was broken out on crossing the line it fouled and did not fill. The crew immediately got busy trying to clear the trouble but tore the sail in doing so and had to haul it in. Meanwhile *Resolute* managed hers very well and began to draw away quickly. Burton decided on desperate measures and set what could only be called a 'jury rig', a sort of flying jib. This was done in very seamanlike manner, a block having to be stopped to the topmast by a seaman aloft to take the halyard. The absence of the balloon sail allowed the jib to set very well and the sail behaved very efficiently, so that *Shamrock* found herself keeping pace with the defender and pointing nearer the mark. Then the breeze changed direction so that *Resolute* now had difficulty in getting her balloon jib to draw and finally abandoned it. *Shamrock* now showed her paces in the light airs and as the wind shifted round the clock each leg of the triangular course became a reach. *Resolute* had no chance now of catching *Shamrock* and it remained to be seen whether the time allowance could be saved. This *Shamrock* did very handsomely, crossing the finishing line nearly ten minutes ahead and winning by two minutes twenty-six seconds on corrected time. The challenger was now two up. All she had to do was to win one more race and the Cup would be back in England.

When the two yachts came out on 21 July excitement was intense both

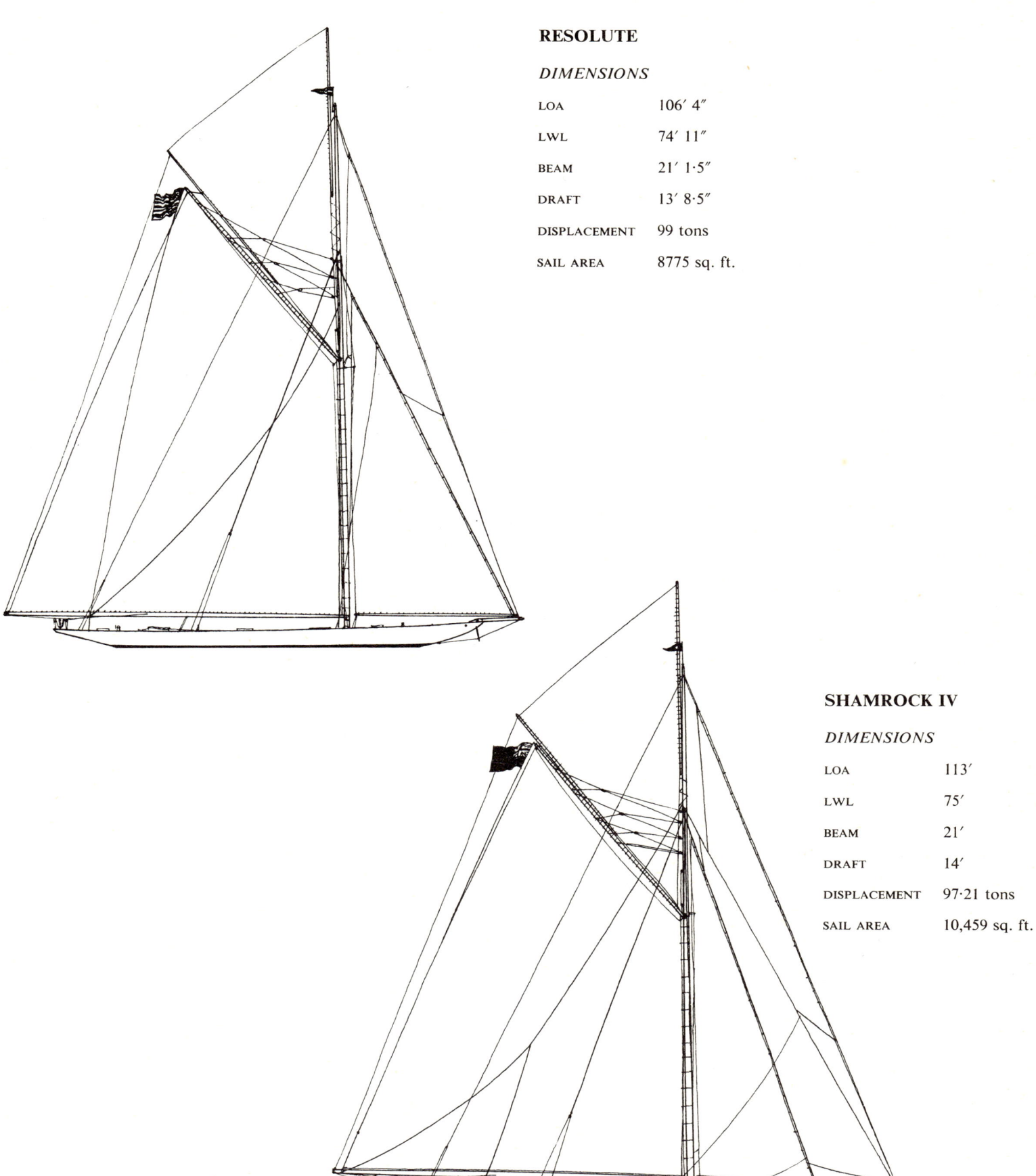

RESOLUTE

DIMENSIONS

LOA	106′ 4″
LWL	74′ 11″
BEAM	21′ 1·5″
DRAFT	13′ 8·5″
DISPLACEMENT	99 tons
SAIL AREA	8775 sq. ft.

SHAMROCK IV

DIMENSIONS

LOA	113′
LWL	75′
BEAM	21′
DRAFT	14′
DISPLACEMENT	97·21 tons
SAIL AREA	10,459 sq. ft.

SERIES	DATE	NAME (winners name first)	COURSE	ELAPSED TIME	CORRECTED TIME	WINS BY	REMARKS
13th	July 15 1920	SHAMROCK IV RESOLUTE	15 miles to windward from Ambrose Channel Lightship and return 30 miles	4.24.58 DID NOT FINISH	4.24.58		
13th	July 20 1920	SHAMROCK IV RESOLUTE	Equilateral triangle from Ambrose Channel Lightship 30 miles	5.22.18 5.31.45	5.22.18 5.24.44	2m 26s	
13th	July 21 1920	RESOLUTE SHAMROCK IV	15 miles to windward from Ambrose Channel Lightship and return 30 miles	4.03.06 4.03.06	3.56.05 4.03.06	7m 01s	
13th	July 23 1920	RESOLUTE SHAMROCK IV	Equilateral triangle from Ambrose Channel Lightship 30 miles	3.37.52 3.41.10	3.31.12 3.41.10	9m 58s	
13th	July 27 1920	RESOLUTE SHAMROCK IV	15 miles to windward from Ambrose Channel Lightship and return 30 miles	5.35.15 5.48.20	5.28.35 5.48.20	19m 45s	

ENTERPRISE

DIMENSIONS

LOA	120′ 9″
LWL	80′
BEAM	21′ 10″
DRAFT	14′ 6″
DISPLACEMENT	128 tons
SAIL AREA	7583 sq. ft.

SHAMROCK V

DIMENSIONS

LOA	119′ 9″
LWL	81′
BEAM	19′ 7·5″
DRAFT	14′ 7″
DISPLACEMENT	134 tons
SAIL AREA	7540 sq. ft.

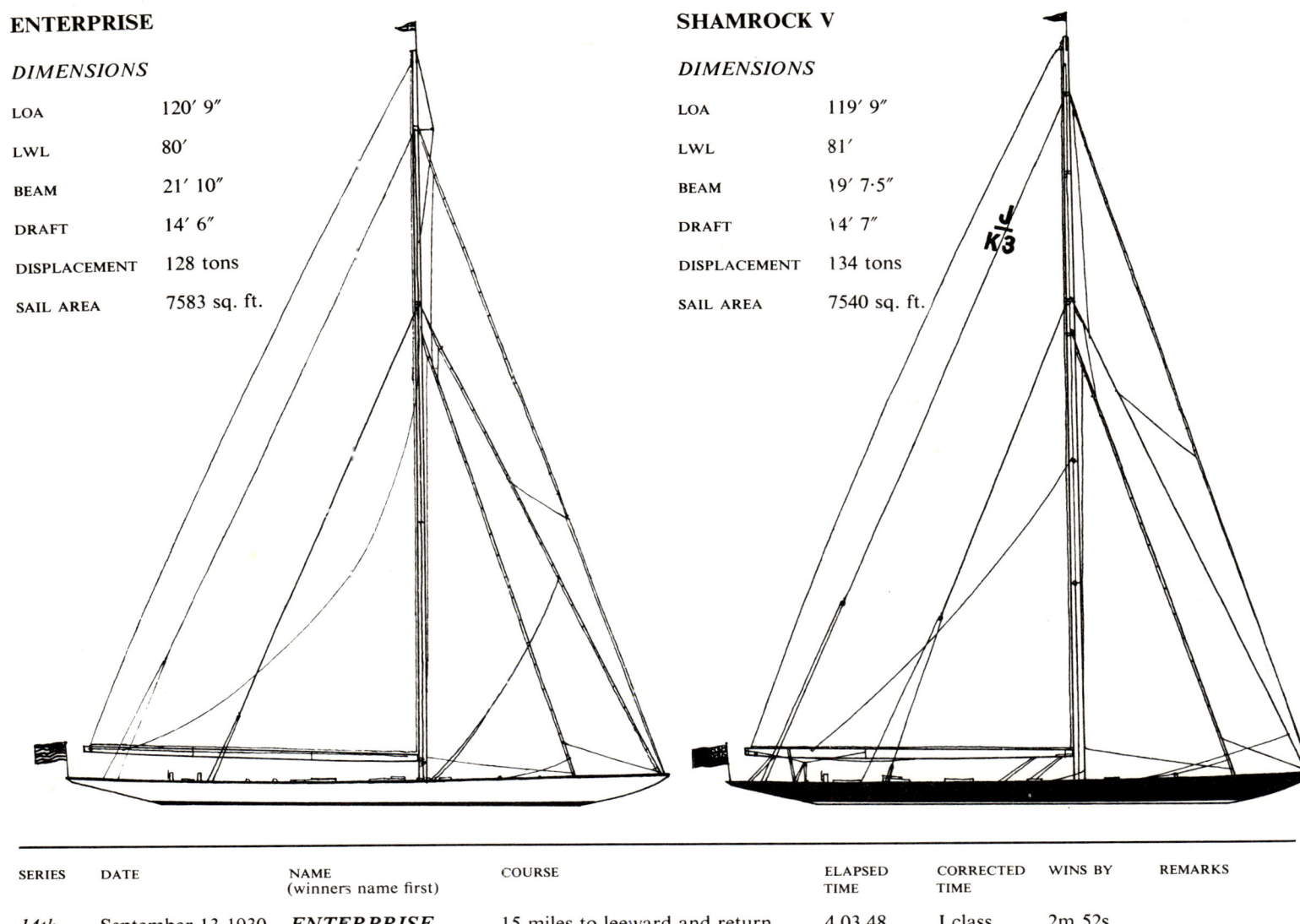

SERIES	DATE	NAME (winners name first)	COURSE	ELAPSED TIME	CORRECTED TIME	WINS BY	REMARKS
14th	September 13 1930	*ENTERPRISE* *SHAMROCK V*	15 miles to leeward and return 30 miles	4.03.48 4.06.40	J class sailed level	2m 52s	
14th	September 15 1930	*ENTERPRISE* *SHAMROCK V*	Equilateral triangle 30 miles	4.00.44 4.10.18		9m 34s	
14th	September 17 1930	*ENTERPRISE* *SHAMROCK V*	15 miles to windward and return 30 miles	3.54.16 DID NOT FINISH			
14th	September 18 1930	*ENTERPRISE* *SHAMROCK V*	Equilateral triangle 30 miles	3.10.13 3.15.57		5m 44s	

in the yachts themselves and in the spectator fleet. Everyone expected a magnificent race and certainly no-one was disappointed. The course was the familiar straight windward and leeward fifteen miles out and back.

It was a fantastic race to follow. *Shamrock* tacked nineteen times on the long beat out, while *Resolute* repeated her former tactics and kept steadily on, as she could point better, and turned the outer mark one minute forty-seven seconds in the lead. The run home was a nightmare for the defender. *Shamrock* steadily gained all the way and when the wind freshened she came bowling along past *Resolute*, drawing well clear, but she ran out of distance and creamed across the line only nineteen seconds in the lead, thus losing on handicap. She wanted another five miles.

Never in all the thirty miles were the two yachts separated by more than a few hundred yards and after this distance had been sailed the timekeepers found that both yachts had taken exactly the same time to sail from the starting line to the finishing line. It was without precedent that two huge yachts such as these should cover the course in exactly four hours thirteen minutes six seconds. *Resolute* took the honours on corrected time winning by seven minutes and one second. The score was now two to one for the challenger.

The next race, on 25 July, was the triangular course. There was a light wind which freshened as time went on. Somehow *Resolute*'s spectacular hair-breadth win seemed to have given her a strangely confident air. People present felt this atmosphere – the sort of feeling which no one can really explain. Adams sailed *Resolute* in a most confident manner, soon leading on the beat on the first leg, and it was clear that his crew were more confident and better altogether. *Shamrock* did everything to match what was obviously an improving team. This was clear to everyone by the number of sail changes made by both yachts with *Resolute*'s crew

matching the seamanship of *Shamrock*. In these conditions Burton rightly tried everything in the book to improve his position whether beating, reaching or running, but *Resolute* replied with exemplary sail-handling and ran out a straight winner by ten minutes on corrected time. Now it was two all.

The next day when the yachts came out the wind was really blowing for the first time, something like twenty-five knots, and both yachts had reefed. Only storm sails were set forward. Nerves were very taut on all counts and it was the Committee's which cracked. They exercised their right to call the race off as in their opinion the lightly constructed yachts were likely to endanger their masts and gear. The decision not only angered the spectator fleet, many of whom were least qualified to comment, but dismayed yachtsmen all over the world. Most people thought this aspect of the contest had been corrected in the decade which had gone by between challenges, yet here again the terms of the Deed of Gift had been flouted. The situation was made even more ironical by one or two large yachts in the spectator fleet standing up firmly in the wind and waves and coming to no harm at all. Yachting correspondents had a busy time writing scathing articles.

The final race was sailed on 27 July in moderate winds. From the start Adams in *Resolute* looked a winner. Burton rightly took every risk and tried everything in the book once again, in the hope of a turn of luck or favourable change of wind, but the faster yacht won when handled by a crew which had reached its peak performance.

So the Cup stayed in America and the world awaited the next challenge, in some doubt as to whether, under the conditions of the Deed, there would ever be another.

It might have been supposed that Sir Thomas Lipton, now getting on in years, would have abandoned all further attempts to 'lift the old mug', but in yachting circles the view was different. There were those who dabbled with the idea themselves, always battling against the difficulty of expense, but in the end the balance, whether to challenge or not, was tipped against doing so out of respect for Sir Thomas's prior claim. This went on for another ten years and then, as had been surmised, in 1929 yet a fifth challenge came from the Royal Ulster Yacht Club on behalf of Sir Thomas Lipton.

It is necessary to dwell for a moment on this challenge, for although it did not add anything very critical to yacht design it not only ended the *Shamrock* era but also changed the rules.

Following very amicable correspondence between Sir Thomas and the New York Yacht Club the latter suggested that they should race with similar yachts of either the J Class (76-foot waterline) or K Class (65-foot waterline) under the Universal Measurements rule and therefore race without any time allowance. Sir Thomas jumped at this proposal which was virtually what he had been advocating all along. He chose the J Class.

This settled, the New York Yacht Club asked him if he would this time agree to racing off Newport, Rhode Island, because of less crowds and shipping and generally more steady and reliable winds. Sir Thomas still did not fall in with this idea readily, as he had rather liked the social side at New York, but as ever he was magnanimous and the Rhode Island approaches were agreed.

The rest of the *Shamrock* story is rather sad. The Americans put up four yachts from which the defender would be chosen, and after the usual series of eliminating races *Enterprise* was chosen, skippered by Harold S. Vanderbilt, and built by W. Starling Burgess, son of Edward of earlier times. Lipton went to Charles E. Nicholson for designer and builder and selected Captain Ted Heard, a professional who had had experience in all previous *Shamrocks*, as skipper.

By mutual consent, the first yacht to win four races took the Cup. There is not much to tell about the racing. *Enterprise* was shown to be clearly the faster of the two yachts and Vanderbilt much the superior helmsman. In fact it was Vanderbilt's unflagging energy in attending to every detail of *Enterprise*'s rig which probably contributed more than anything else to the American victory. The sliding-foot boom, the lighter mast and sails and the exhaustive experiments during trials, with the ever present problem of the luffs setting perfectly, showed application to the task which may have been equalled in later years but never bettered.

Sir Thomas Lipton had not 'lifted the old mug'. But he had lifted the greatest yacht competition to the heights which the original donors had hoped to achieve. Unhappily he was failing in mind and sometimes did not seem to know fully what was going on, so that when at long last the Royal Yacht Squadron made him a member this honour, which would have meant so much to him a few years earlier, in some respects passed him by.

CHAPTER 7

Endeavour

The story now moves on to the next decade and an exciting period in the America's Cup history. In 1933 a challenge was received by the New York Yacht Club from the Royal Yacht Squadron on behalf of Mr T. O. M. Sopwith (later Sir Thomas Sopwith). The challenger was designed and built by Charles E. Nicholson of Gosport and was named *Endeavour*. She was the best British J Class yacht of her day.

Sopwith had every qualification for undertaking a challenge. His aircraft firm, dating from the First World War, had taught him much in the field of light metals. He had done well sailing twelve-metre yachts in the late 'twenties and he had bought and raced *Shamrock V*. There was a special interest in the Sopwith challenge because he was to be the first owner skipper contesting for the Cup.

This series was notable for many things but firstly for a revolution in sails. Jib topsails disappeared and genoa jibs came in. The double clew jib designed by Sopwith made its appearance in company with double luff spinnakers. This double clew jib was spotted by the Americans while being tested in the Solent and was copied by them in time to supply it to the defender, thus greatly helping her performance.

All negotiations were carried out through the Royal Yacht Squadron, on behalf of Sopwith, throughout the *Endeavour* series. The first of these was agreed to be raced off Newport and the yacht first winning four out of seven races would take the Cup.

The Americans stuck to the old firm to defend. Vanderbilt was named as manager/skipper and Herreshoff's yard was commissioned to build a defender to the design of Starling Burgess. The yacht was named *Rainbow*.

There was however a yacht, the *Yankee*, skippered by Frank Paine, which wished to contend for the honour of defending, and the eliminating races showed that *Rainbow* was not necessarily the fastest yacht but that, in the opinion of the selection committee, *Rainbow* had the best skipper and leader and this probably tipped the scales in making the selection.

There are those who believe that *Yankee* should have been defending, and had not the eliminating trials been ended rather abruptly by the Committee, *Yankee* would have been able to claim the honour. She was a Boston yacht and had she conclusively proved her superiority over *Rainbow*, Frank Paine would have had to become a member of the New York Yacht Club in order to defend. It will be remembered that this situation had occurred with Mr Lawson, owner of the Boston yacht *Independence* in 1901, and the embarrassing situation had been saved by Mr Lawson's yacht not being good enough. In this case *Yankee* and Frank Paine were possibly the best combination, but it could be that the Committee were influenced in their decision to select a New York Yacht Club boat and skipper by considerations other than those solely of yachting.

While the Americans had two needle-sharp yachts ready at their disposal, *Endeavour I* on the other hand experienced crew trouble, as over half went on strike for higher wages. Sopwith told the professional crew that they could come on the original and agreed terms or not at all. About two-thirds opted to stay at home. There was a rush to fill the vacancies and, within a few days, applications from a thousand yachtsmen had been received.*

This presented him with a real problem but the selection was made for him by the Commodore of the Royal Corinthian Yacht Club, literally over the weekend. Sopwith sailed for America with a crew one-third professional and two-thirds amateur.

Before the first race both boats were dry docked, which revealed *Endeavour* to be all steel, while *Rainbow* was bronze below the waterline with steel above.

Not unexpectedly a good deal of talent was mustered in each yacht. Vanderbilt took with him Starling Burgess and Sherman Hoyt, the latter a man of considerable big yacht experience and a wizard in light airs. Sopwith had with him Mrs Sopwith as timekeeper, Charles Nicholson the designer and builder and Frank Murdock who had designed nearly all the rig.

The first race was abandoned after the wind had died out, when both boats were within a short distance of the finish but with *Rainbow* leading. The day was remarkable for the size of the spectator fleet. It was said that as many as 10,000 people had managed to get afloat.

The first completed race took place on 17 September and as usual was a course of fifteen miles out and back. There was a good strong breeze and *Endeavour* showed her paces all the way getting home the winner by two minutes nine seconds. The next day conditions were very similar and this time it was the triangular course. Again *Endeavour* showed she was the faster yacht and won by fifty-one seconds, a margin which would have been bigger if her mixed crew had had more working-up time. Also amateur hands are not as hard as those of professionals and already some were blistering and showing signs of wear. Both yachts beat the record for this course previously held by *Enterprise*.

With two up, *Endeavour* seemed to be within sight of the Cup. When the third race started on 20 September it was the fifteen miles out and back course with the first leg a straight run down wind. *Endeavour* sailed gloriously away from the defender and rounded the seaward mark six minutes twenty-three seconds ahead, apparently set for a clear win. At this point Vanderbilt went below having turned the helm over to Sherman Hoyt, at the same time remarking that the Cup was as good as back in England. Then suddenly the wind played a fateful trick and changed the whole course of events. Firstly instead of a true beat home with a fair wind, it became a tricky sail in light airs. In this duel *Rainbow*'s genoa became an important factor for the simple reason that Sopwith did not have a corresponding sail, as his had been split at the clew in a previous race. He had to make do with a balloon jib which was not really suitable for a beat so close to the wind in very light airs and in any case it was a borrowed sail. So to the astonishment of all, *Rainbow* gradually came up on *Endeavour*. Sopwith tacked to keep ahead of his rival, intending to stand on *Rainbow*'s weather, but these two turns tended to take the weigh

---

* The numbers of crew in challengers racing in American waters have always been guided by rules, and in the case of the J Class the number was 31. The earlier yachts, particularly some of the very big ones, had more, and in some cases there were restrictive rules. Latterly, in the 12-metres, crews have numbered ten or eleven — in these days, with very sophisticated spinnakers, generally eleven. There are rules governing these numbers, and crews are limited to three and one additional person for each 13.23 square metres of rated sail area and they have to be amateurs.

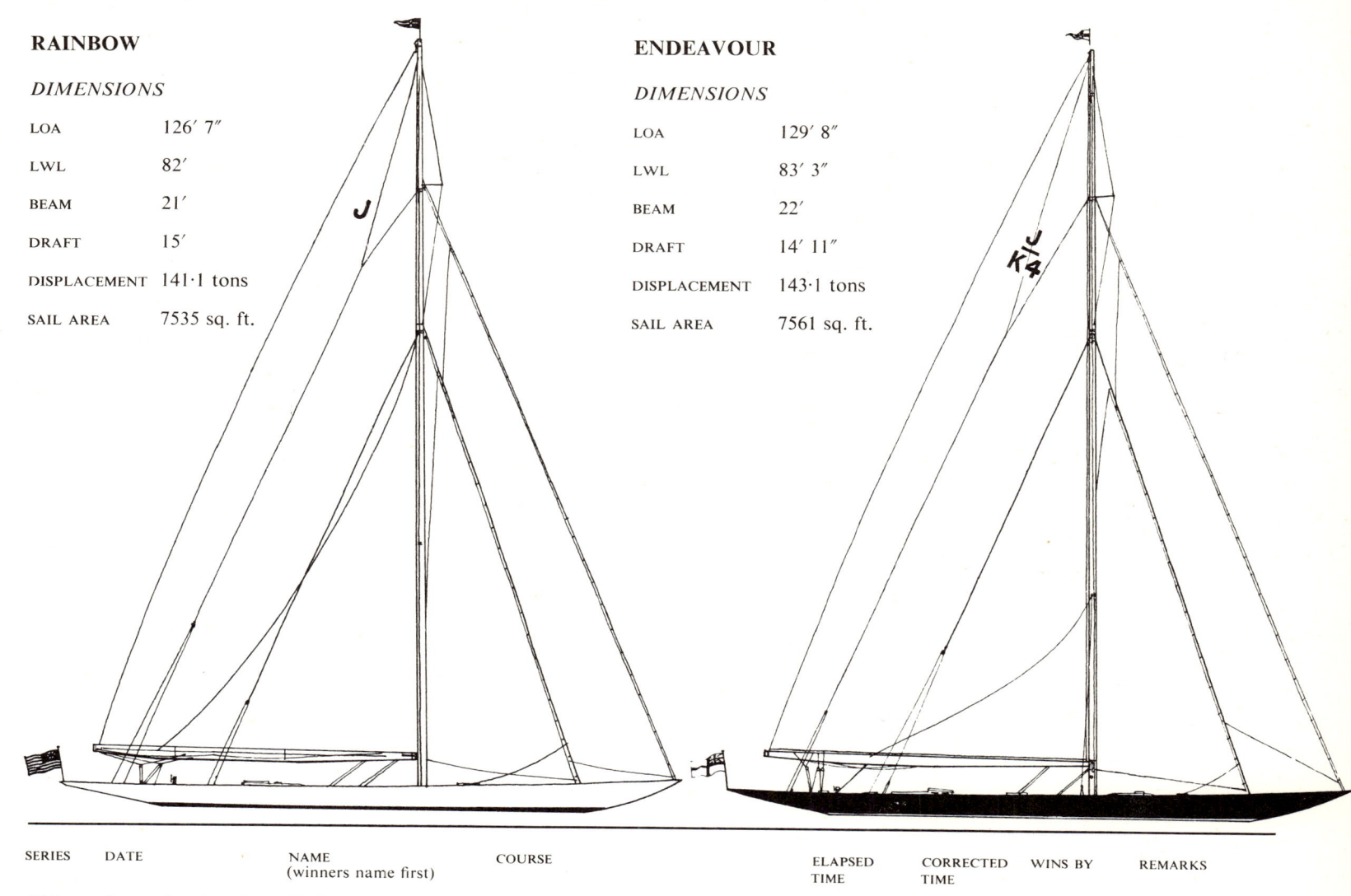

RAINBOW

DIMENSIONS

LOA	126′ 7″
LWL	82′
BEAM	21′
DRAFT	15′
DISPLACEMENT	141·1 tons
SAIL AREA	7535 sq. ft.

ENDEAVOUR

DIMENSIONS

LOA	129′ 8″
LWL	83′ 3″
BEAM	22′
DRAFT	14′ 11″
DISPLACEMENT	143·1 tons
SAIL AREA	7561 sq. ft.

SERIES	DATE	NAME (winners name first)	COURSE	ELAPSED TIME	CORRECTED TIME	WINS BY	REMARKS
15th	September 17 1934	*ENDEAVOUR* *RAINBOW*	15 miles to windward and return *30 miles*	3.43.44 3.45.53	J class sailed level	2m 09s	
15th	September 18 1934	*ENDEAVOUR* *RAINBOW*	Equilateral triangle *30 miles*	3.09.01 3.09.52		0m 51s	
15th	September 20 1934	*RAINBOW* *ENDEAVOUR*	15 miles to leeward and return *30 miles*	4.35.34 4.39.00		3m 26s	
15th	September 22 1934	*RAINBOW* *ENDEAVOUR*	Equilateral triangle *30 miles*	3.15.38 3.16.53		1m 15s	
15th	September 24 1934	*RAINBOW* *ENDEAVOUR*	15 miles to leeward and return *30 miles*	3.54.05 3.58.06		4m 01s	
15th	September 25 1934	*RAINBOW* *ENDEAVOUR*	Equilateral triangle *30 miles*	3.40.05 3.41.00		0m 55s	

off the yacht and *Rainbow*, now being brilliantly sailed by Sherman Hoyt, ghosted through to take the lead which *Endeavour* was unable to regain. *Rainbow* crossed the line the winner by three minutes twenty-six seconds.

Sopwith is quite open and magnanimous about this. 'We made a mistake,' he says, and what yachtsman has never done that? Had he borne away a trifle, thereby making the best use of his balloon jib and disregarded *Rainbow*, he would have won, because the wind unexpectedly veered making the second half of this leg suitable for the balloon jib. In fact *Endeavour* could have laid the mark without a tack.

The score was now 2:1 and Vanderbilt, recognising his good fortune in the last race, knew that if he was to win another, something more had to be done. *Endeavour* had outsailed *Rainbow* particularly well on the runs. If Vanderbilt was to avoid going down in history as the first man to lose the Cup, this something had to be drastic. In this desperate situation he took the only course open to him and telephoned Frank Paine in Boston. This magnanimous yachtsman did not hesitate and decided his best contribution would be to come himself bringing *Yankee*'s spinnaker with him. Vanderbilt also had two more tons of ballast put on board which took him to the limit of the rating, in the hope that this would improve *Rainbow*'s performance. This was a thoughtful experiment which paid dividends.

The next race was over the triangular course and the whole day was full of incident as might have been expected. Firstly there was some knife-edge manoeuvring at the start which the experts in the Committee boat followed with intense interest and concentration. Then on the first leg, for the first ten miles, the yachts kept close together with *Rainbow* leading, but not by a sufficient margin to prevent *Endeavour* covering *Rainbow*'s weather quarter to such a point that, when the first mark was reached, Vanderbilt could not round it, since if he had put his helm over he would have fouled the challenger. Sopwith carried him some way past the mark and then went about. Vanderbilt followed at once and in the drill for setting the genoas *Rainbow* was the quicker and Sopwith saw his yacht being overtaken for the second time. Instantly therefore he decided to luff and as he did so he realised that Vanderbilt was not going to respond.

The rules at that time said that if a yacht was being overtaken to windward she could luff her opponent provided she could, if she held her luff, strike the other yacht forward of the mast. Thus this vital matter was left in the hands of two men both clutching desperately at the most coveted yachting trophy in the world. Sopwith was sure he would have struck forward of the mast. Vanderbilt thought differently and held his course. Sopwith could have forced a collision but what use would that have been? A collision between two such magnificent yachts was unthinkable. So he bore away. *Rainbow* ran on, rounding the second mark in the lead, and on the final run home Frank Paine and his spinnaker settled the issue, except that *Endeavour* was seen to be flying a protest flag.

The next day was a Sunday and the Committee considered two protests by Sopwith. The first concerned manoeuvring at the start and the second the luffing incident. The Committee refused to hear either protest. Remarking on the jockeying at the start, the Committee stated that they had observed an incident themselves which would have disqualified *Endeavour*, not *Rainbow*. All the same it is for the opponent to protest, and Vanderbilt in *Rainbow* had not done so. Regarding the other and vital matter of the luffing incident, the Committee quoted the rule which stated that 'a protest must be made at the time of the incident'. While this was true for the New York Yacht Club, the custom at that time in English yachting circles was to protest to the Committee. So the protest flag was not shown until the Committee boat was in sight; in this case at the time of the incident it was fifteen miles away. Mr C. F. Havemeyer, the representative of the New York Yacht Club on board *Endeavour*, agreed with Sopwith to withhold hoisting the flag on this consideration. Also privately Sopwith felt, quite rightly, that he still might win the race – thus eliminating the need to protest and, as no protest had been made since 1895 during the *Dunraven* affair, this reasoning was both generous and justified. Understandably the whole of the English crew were dumb-founded and the atmosphere of the series became strained.

So the yachts came out for the fifth race under tension. This time the course was the fifteen miles out and back. Both made good starts but *Rainbow* was quicker with her spinnaker and just got the edge. In earlier races *Endeavour*, once she had got going, would have come past the defender whether running or beating and made certain of winning, but this time, on the run, *Rainbow* kept her lead and increased it with every mile. There is little doubt that this was due partly to Frank Paine and his spinnaker and partly to the extra ballast.

There was one moment on this run which could have cost *Rainbow* the race. In the confusion of setting a new spinnaker a man was knocked overboard but managed to hold on to the halyard and was hoisted inboard again in a matter of seconds. Had he fallen clean over the side *Rainbow* would have had to pick him up and ended her chances of winning. The beat home was without incident and *Rainbow* won by some four minutes.

Now *Rainbow* led by three races to two and it was a sad crew which sailed *Endeavour* to the starting line for the last race. But all was by no means over. As soon as the yachts, as ever close together, had crossed the line with *Endeavour* slightly in the lead, Sopwith luffed and this time Vanderbilt responded, going about to do so. *Endeavour* again showed her paces on the beat, reaching the first mark more than a minute ahead. Not long afterwards *Rainbow* tacked and Sopwith would normally have covered but *Endeavour* had a 'mix up' forward with a jib hank fouling both stays which took nearly twenty minutes to clear. The delay this caused enabled *Rainbow* to take advantage of a slight change in the direction of the wind and point to the buoy while *Endeavour* had to tack. Thus *Rainbow* rounded the second mark with two minutes forty-five seconds in hand. On the run home this time Frank Paine did not seem to hold the magic wand any longer and *Endeavour* came up on her rival all the way, but as in one of the *Shamrock* races she ran out of distance and the finishing line was crossed with the challenger fifty-five seconds astern.

It is important to record that a careful study of the photographs of the luffing incident in the fourth race shows clearly that when *Endeavour* had borne away after the luff, the two yachts were parallel; and even a second luff at this later stage would have been correct. In support of this,

Sherman Hoyt later gave it as his opinion that Sopwith's luff was positioned correctly and the protest should have been sustained, a very responsible opinion by a man who was in the defender at the time. Perhaps, though, a fair portion of the blame may be laid on Havemeyer, of the New York Yacht Club, who agreed with Sopwith not to hoist the protest flag at the time, though he must have known that failure to do so would very probably jeopardise the protest.

In the last two races there is little doubt that Vanderbilt's crew, composed chiefly of experienced Scandinavians, had the measure of Sopwith's amateurs who did everything crew could be expected to achieve, but in the final races they were hauling sheets with the raw flesh of their hands. The advice of Frank Paine, and the ballast adjustment, also greatly improved the defender's performance. These three factors gave Vanderbilt sufficient advantage to hold off the challenge in the remaining races.

In spite of all the disappointment, that great-hearted and magnanimous owner/skipper, Tommy Sopwith, saw to it that he left the States with friendship restored in great measure and a promise to try and come back one day. There were more than 1000 people at the final dinner given by the New York Yacht Club, a gesture to Sopwith unmistakable in its warmth and intention.

CHAPTER 8

Try Again

True to his word Sopwith commissioned Charles Nicholson to build another yacht. The result was the fastest J Class ever built on this side of the Atlantic. Nicholson went to the limit of dimensions for the class and gave her an 87-foot waterline.

Trials and races in 1936 ironed out the troubles, the major one being the 5500-pound steel mast, which was not strong enough to carry the area of sail allowed, so a mast of 6300 pounds was substituted.

By midsummer of 1936 Sopwith was satisfied that his new yacht *Endeavour II* was faster than *Endeavour I*, and the expected challenge was made.

From the experience of the 1934 races it was clear that the Americans would have to build a new defender and, after appointing Vanderbilt as skipper, the Committee of the New York Yacht Club on the advice of the usual Vanderbilt turned to Starling Burgess for their design, but with one additional collaborator.

At the age of twenty-nine, Olin J. Stevens had already begun to make his name in yacht design. Realising that everything had to be done to produce a defender which would match the challenger, the Committee, again advised by Vanderbilt, invited Stevens to join the design team. If the choice of Charlie Barr as skipper in days gone by had been a good piece of crystal gazing, the bringing in of Olin Stevens to the design team was nothing short of brilliant. The result of the dual skills of Burgess and Stevens was *Ranger*, the fastest J Class yacht ever built, and one which some say would never have been matched so long as the Js remained the accepted class for the America's Cup races.

It will be remembered that G. L. Watson first took to tank-testing model yachts, but his were early days. In 1937 Stevens had the advantage of the Stevens Institute of Technology under the able directorship of Professor Kenneth Davidson. In the tank in this Institute testing had been developed which produced all the answers in all conditions of wind strength, heel, waves and with all types of hull. Burgess and Stevens made models of *Enterprise, Rainbow* and *Endeavour I*, the last being made possible by the typical if misguided generosity of Charles Nicholson. This kindness was a pity, but it is extremely doubtful even if Nicholson had not been so forthcoming, whether it would have made any difference. From that time to this day Olin Stevens has remained the outstanding large racing-yacht designer. The secret of his work is in the hulls, and particularly of *Ranger*, which could carry a greater sail area than any other yacht for a given force of wind, while still retaining the designed angle of heel for maximum efficiency.

There was a hold-up on the American side because of lack of finance, as no syndicate could be formed. Everyone in the New York Yacht Club said 'leave it to Vanderbilt', and this is how it stood for some time until Vanderbilt decided to 'go it alone'. It was he who chose the name *Ranger*, after the famous man-o'-war captained by Paul Jones which, on 14 February 1778 in Quiberon Bay, received the first salute to the American flag from a foreign country.

Ranger was built at the Bath Iron Works in Maine. She was made of steel and was the first yacht to defend the Cup which had not been built in Herreshoff's yard since 1890.

Although *Ranger* was not unique, in that she lost a mast when under tow on her way to the fitting out yard, due to strain on the steel shrouds under excessive roll, she was exceptional in most other respects. She won twelve eliminating races straight off the reel and then, because the crew did not want their first defence of the Cup to be their thirteenth race, *Ranger* took part in a club race and beat all comers with ease. It should be added that *Ranger* had a double clew genoa in her locker, a development of Sopwith's double clew jib, which she was able to carry owing to her remarkable stability.

On 31 July 1937 *Endeavour* and *Ranger* came out to the starting line nine miles south-east of the Brenton Reef light vessel. They had a job to see their ways clear, as some eight hundred spectator craft of all kinds had also made the trip. It was nearly an hour in the light breeze before the coastguards had made a sufficient clearance. The course was the usual fifteen-mile out-and-back opening round. Sopwith got slightly the better of the start. Vanderbilt tacked to clear his wind from *Endeavour*'s favourable position and, although Sopwith covered the tack, *Ranger* began to show her paces as soon as she had the true wind. For sail-changing this beat to the outer mark must have been a strenuous exercise for *Endeavour*'s crew who showed admirable seamanship and moved fast, but nothing which Sopwith could do made any impression on the defender. *Ranger* reached the buoy marking the outer fifteen-mile turning point 6 minutes 14 seconds ahead.

Now the wind shifted a couple of points making the homeward leg more of a reach than a run. *Ranger* just continued to go ahead finishing the winner by 17 minutes 5 seconds. For Sopwith, with the fastest J Class yacht ever built in European waters, this was a shock, the more so because he had made no mistakes and had sailed *Endeavour* with undoubted skill. Fifty years had gone by since a challenger had suffered such a beating. Charles Nicholson was openly amazed and well he might have been.

The next day the yachts went off on the triangular course and again Sopwith out-manoeuvred Vanderbilt, this time getting by far the better of the start, and then proceeded to hold him in *Endeavour*'s back wind for something over an hour. Eventually Vanderbilt bore away and should have been left nicely astern, but he was able to make such pace, once in the true wind, that he took *Ranger* ten minutes ahead and the other two legs of the triangle only added to the lead, *Ranger* winning by 18 minutes and 32 seconds.

Two more races were sailed, one over the 15-mile out-and-back course and the final over the triangular course. In these two races *Ranger* suffered some mistakes in drill and Sopwith took every advantage of them, particularly in the last race when he initiated a tacking duel which his crew won in sail-handling, but it was to no avail. *Ranger* won both races, although with less margins, possibly because Nicholson removed some ballast from *Endeavour* which seemed to make her a trifle faster, so that Sopwith held *Ranger* at times during the final race, but not for sufficiently long to cause anxiety to the defender.

The answer to all this lay in the magic of Olin Stevens. His genius was acknowledged by all, including Vanderbilt, who turned over the helm to Olin in the last race a mile or two from home, so that he could skipper the yacht across the finishing line.

RANGER

DIMENSIONS

LOA	135' 2"
LWL	87'
BEAM	20' 11"
DRAFT	15'
DISPLACEMENT	166 tons
SAIL AREA	7546 sq. ft.

ENDEAVOUR II

DIMENSIONS

LOA	135' 9·5"
LWL	86' 6"
BEAM	21' 6"
DRAFT	15'
DISPLACEMENT	162·6 tons
SAIL AREA	7543 sq. ft.

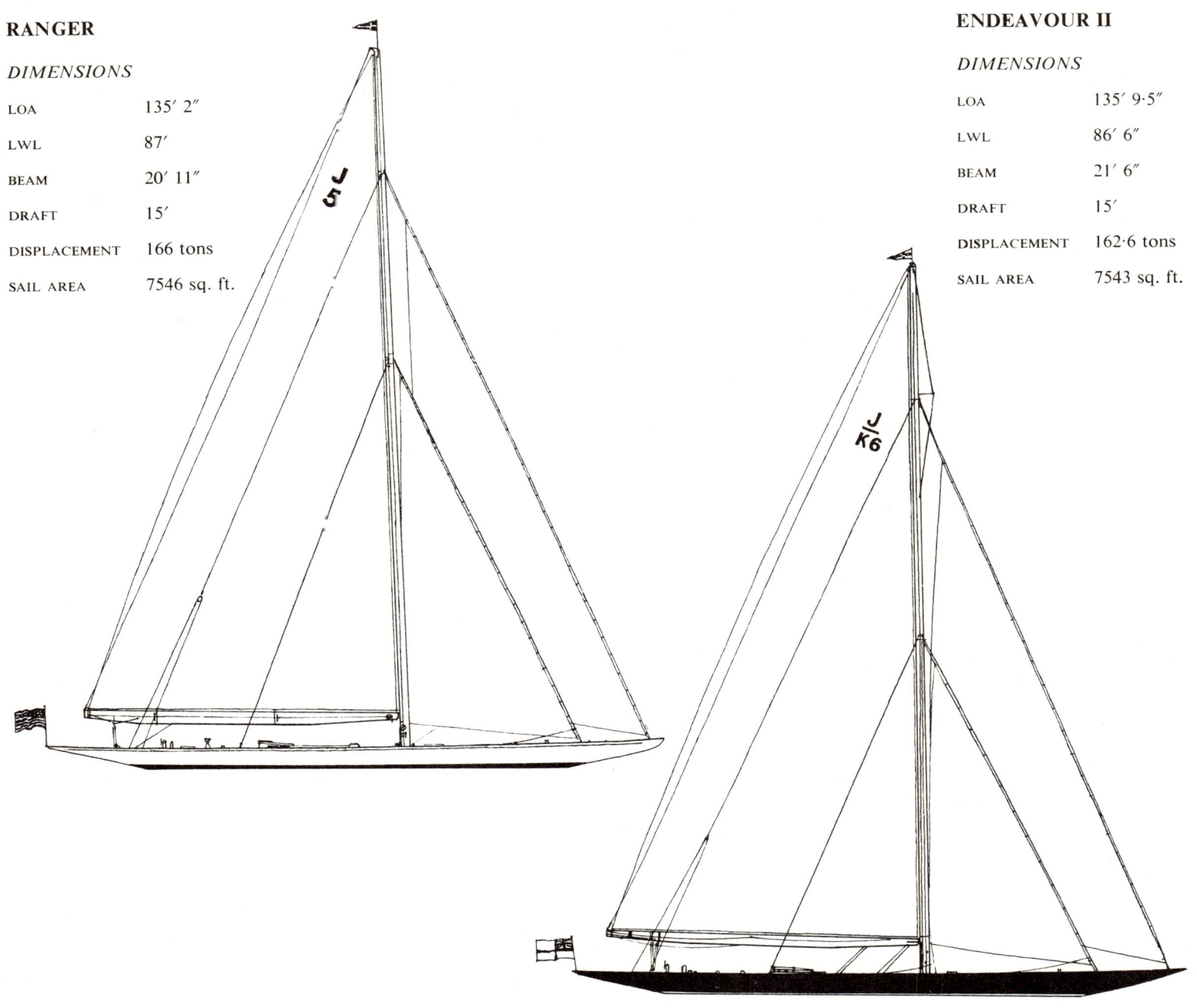

SERIES	DATE	NAME (winners name first)	COURSE	ELAPSED TIME	CORRECTED TIME	WINS BY	REMARKS
16th	July 31 1937	*RANGER* *ENDEAVOUR II*	15 miles to windward and return *30 miles*	4.41.15 4.58.20	J class sailed level	17m 05s	
16th	August 2 1937	*RANGER* *ENDEAVOUR II*	Equilateral triangle *30 miles*	3.41.33 4.00.05		˙18m 32s	
16th	August 4 1937	*RANGER* *ENDEAVOUR II*	15 miles to windward and return *30 miles*	3.54.30 3.58.57		4m 27s	
16th	August 5 1937	*RANGER* *ENDEAVOUR II*	Equilateral triangle *30 miles*	3.07.49 3.11.26		3m 37s	

As competition the series had been disappointing but, with the obvious superiority of *Ranger*, almost from the first moment, the atmosphere was relaxed and there was a spirit of friendship and mutual respect throughout which made this an enjoyable contest for all concerned.

Sopwith was invited to stay on and take part in some of the summer cruises, racing along the American seaboard, which he gladly accepted. There was much good fun on this holiday tour and when it ended *Ranger* had won twelve races and was second in one. *Endeavour* had chalked up seven second-places in some good racing in which the two America's Cup contestants were joined by *Rainbow* and *Yankee*. No one could hold *Ranger*, easily the fastest J Class yacht ever built.

It would have set British designers and yachtsmen a massive task to work out a better challenger for the next series, but the Second World War intervened, and the question of whether anyone could have produced a faster yacht than *Ranger* remains unanswered for all time, for *Ranger* did not survive the war, being broken up for scrap.

CHAPTER 9

The First of the Twelves

The First World War reduced the potential challengers in big yachts for the America's Cup to a handful of dedicated yachtsmen, and the Second World War eliminated them altogether. In consequence twenty years went by before the next challenge was made, yet again by the Royal Yacht Squadron, but not on behalf of one man. As the Americans had done many times in the past, a syndicate was formed. Before this part of the story can be told it is necessary to bridge the gap between the last challenge in 1937 and this first post-war challenge in 1957.

After the *Endeavour II* series in 1937 two years passed under the shadows of gathering war clouds. The next seven were spent in open conflict and its immediate aftermath. Then from 1946 to 1956 there followed a period when enthusiasts searched for a means of reopening the greatest yachting competition in the world.

By the last Deed of Gift the yachts had to have a minimum waterline of 65 feet and it was obvious to all that this ruling would have to be changed. Even American syndicates could no longer afford yachts of this size, let alone a group of Englishmen. All manner of suggestions were made by leading yachtsmen on both sides of the Atlantic, notably on the English side by Captain John Illingworth, a world renowned yacht builder and designer besides being a leading racing helmsman and playing an important part in initiating some of the ocean races of post-war times. Suggestions ranged from long-distance ocean contests to inshore 14-foot dinghy races, but on close examination none of these ideas came sufficiently close to the terms of the Deed to be acceptable. However, both Americans and Englishmen were determined to find a solution and after much friendly discussion the New York Yacht Club took the matter to the Supreme Court. They requested a ruling to reduce the waterline length of yachts to 45 feet. This could only be a Supreme Court decision because the last of the original custodians of the Deed had died, and therefore it was no longer possible to return the Cup and ask for a new Deed to suit modern needs.

The Supreme Court found in favour of the 45-foot waterline length and the stage was set for the reopening of the America's Cup competition. The yacht which answered the new length and the remaining existing conditions more nearly than any other was the standard 12-metre, and although this type of yacht could perfectly well cross the Atlantic on its own bottom, by mutual consent this condition was waived.

So it was that in June 1957 the next challenge was sent from England, and immediately on both sides of the Atlantic minds were concentrated on 12-metre design. In this the Americans had the advantage from the past on which to build, because in 1939 Harold S. Vanderbilt brought over to England a 12-metre yacht called *Vim*. This yacht, designed by Olin Stevens, made racing history with a phenomenal record of wins and an outstanding crew.

The English syndicate was formed by H. A. Andreae, Bertram Currie, Hugh L. Goodson, Group-Captain Loel Guinness, Major Harold W. Hall, Sir Peter W. Hoare, Major MacDonald-Buchanan, Viscount Runciman, C. B. C. Wainman, Viscount Camrose and Sir John Wardlaw-Milne. Hugh Goodson was the Chairman. This formidable list illustrated clearly what people on this side of the Atlantic considered necessary in yachting talent and financial strength to support a challenge in these post-war times.

These gentlemen were utterly determined to make a first-class showing in the seventeenth series and commissioned four designers to submit two designs each. The designers were David Boyd, James McGruer, Charles Nicholson (Junior) and Arthur C. Robb. They were asked to produce one conventional 12-metre design and one of an advanced order. Thus the syndicate had eight models to take to the testing tank at Saunders Roe in the Isle of Wight. The tests were completed by July 1957. The choice was a most difficult one and infinite trouble was taken both by the Saunders Roe experts and by the syndicate. It was the advanced design submitted by David Boyd which was selected, and construction was put in hand immediately at the yard of Messrs Robertsons of Sandbank in Scotland, which was in fact David Boyd's yard.

Sceptre, as the yacht was called, was launched in April 1958 and as soon as she was completed began her trials and working-up. The trial horse was *Evaine*, considered the best existing 12-metre and which Mr Owen Aisher, another noted English yachtsman, generously purchased and modernised. Here it should be added that members of the syndicate also put their hands in their pockets generously and frequently, so that *Sceptre* would lack nothing.

The day came when *Sceptre* and *Evaine* met for the first time and memories went back to 1939 when *Vim* had come over to England and had soundly defeated *Evaine* in every race. Therefore if *Sceptre* was to be a hopeful challenger she must beat *Evaine* easily. Of course allowance had to be made for a yacht which was racing for the very first time, but when *Evaine* won the first trial, matters looked serious.

Gradually, during the summer, *Sceptre* gained ascendancy over *Evaine*, but the degree of superiority was too small for rejoicing. There was even talk of withdrawing the challenge, but this would have been a very big thing to do bearing in mind that no less than four American yachts were working-up for their eliminating trials.

The American yachts were *Columbia*, designed by Olin Stevens for a syndicate headed by Henry Sears; *Vim*, of Olin Stevens's design, refurbished into splendid condition by John N. Mathews; *Weatherly*, designed by Phil Rhodes for a syndicate headed by Henry Mercer, and *Easterner*, designed by C. Raymond Hunt for a syndicate headed by Chandler Hovey. *Easterner* was really a family affair with Chandler Hovey the principal owner. With three new yachts and the reconditioned Olin Stevens masterpiece *Vim* against her, *Sceptre* had a long way to go.

The challenger arrived at Newport, Rhode Island, just as the American eliminating trials were beginning in August. Her good and talented crew were to witness and hear fascinating details of some of the finest 12-metre racing ever to take place. Commander Graham Mann, her helmsman, Commander Joe Brooks, the navigator, Colin Ratsey (Senior), relief helmsman, and Stan Brooks (no better professional to be in charge of the hands), sensed and saw the tremendous opposition which had been mustered against them.

The American eliminating races went on until 11 September, just on a whole month's racing. They deserve a chapter on their own, but to describe them in full is not the purpose of this book. At the end of every day's racing, improvements were brought in for sails, sail-handling and helming, and tactics were discussed well into the night. During August, *Weatherly*, helmed by Arthur Knapp, *Vim* in the hands of 'Bus'

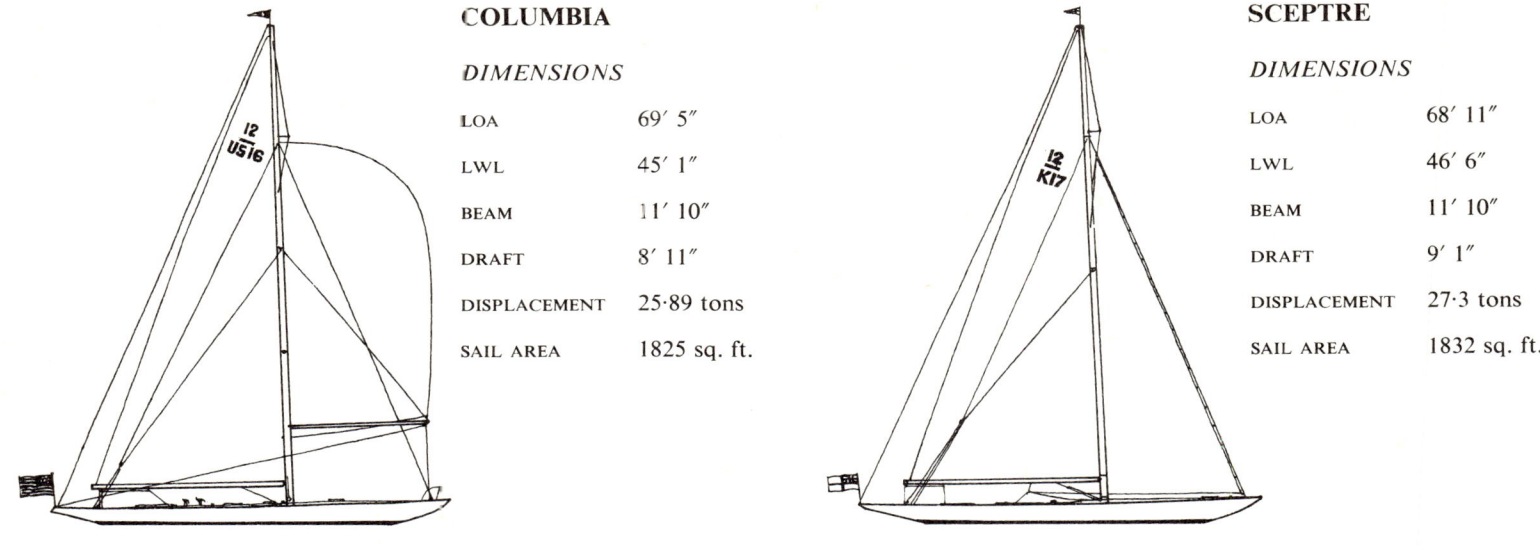

	COLUMBIA			SCEPTRE	
	DIMENSIONS			**DIMENSIONS**	
	LOA	69' 5"		LOA	68' 11"
	LWL	45' 1"		LWL	46' 6"
	BEAM	11' 10"		BEAM	11' 10"
	DRAFT	8' 11"		DRAFT	9' 1"
	DISPLACEMENT	25·89 tons		DISPLACEMENT	27·3 tons
	SAIL AREA	1825 sq. ft.		SAIL AREA	1832 sq. ft.

SERIES	DATE	NAME (winners name first)	COURSE	ELAPSED TIME	CORRECTED TIME	WINS BY	REMARKS
17th	September 20 1958	*COLUMBIA* *SCEPTRE*	6 miles to windward and return Twice round *24 miles*	5.13.56 5.21.40	12-metre sailed level	7m 44s	
17th	September 24 1958	*COLUMBIA* *SCEPTRE*	Equilateral triangle *24 miles*	3.17.43 3.29.25		11m 42s	
17th	September 25 1958	*COLUMBIA* *SCEPTRE*	6 miles to windward and return Twice round *24 miles*	2.59.07 3.07.27		8m 20s	
17th	September 26 1958	*COLUMBIA* *SCEPTRE*	Equilateral triangle *24 miles*	3.04.22 3.11.27		7m 05s	*SCEPTRE* broke main boom

Mosbacher, and *Columbia* skippered and helmed by Briggs Cunningham with Olin Stevens as relief, proved to be better all round than *Easterner*. Of the other three, neither the Committee of the New York Yacht Club nor the experts among the general yachting fraternity could make up their minds. *Weatherly* at this point was perhaps the favourite. All her crew were splendid and her spinnaker was particularly good, but she did not hold this coveted position and by the end of the first week in September *Columbia* and *Vim* had shown a definite superiority over her.

It really looked as though *Vim*, the old campaigner, might be selected. Still undecided the Committee ordered another round of races and of these *Columbia* came out fractionally the better. When *Sceptre*'s crew heard of the choice they were in fact a little relieved not to be sailing against *Vim*. Not only did *Vim* have a terrifying reputation for winning, but her crew when on their metal were magnificent.

Sceptre's working-up races were unhappily a totally different affair. With only the experience of racing against *Evaine*, a yacht known not to be as good as *Vim*, she needed hard racing against first-class opposition. Sadly, the only yacht available to help was *Gleam*, which was generously lent by her American owner. Not only was *Gleam* twenty-one years old but she was fitted with an engine and therefore had to trail the screw. Owen Aisher and a willing crew did their best, but poor *Sceptre* sometimes had to drag buckets over the stern to make a match or alternatively Owen Aisher ran the engine to leg along faster.

Before the first race on 20 September, *Columbia* was offered and accepted the pick of the other three yachts' sails and gear, while all that *Sceptre* could do was to go over every point in the American eliminating trials, which members of the English team had followed in every detail, so that they would have a full knowledge of their opponents' tactics when the real racing began.

Whatever was to come, one success had already been achieved. Both crews were predominantly amateurs, and from the very first meetings a most friendly atmosphere prevailed. This was carried further to the owners of both yachts as a number of the Royal Yacht Squadron syndicate had come over. There was even some integration in the crews, because Colin Ratsey in *Columbia*'s crew was the nephew of Colin Ratsey (Senior) in *Sceptre*. For good measure it is worth a note that Halsey Herreshoff in *Columbia* was a nephew of the famous Nat.

The first race was as usual the straight windward-leeward course, twice round, making a total distance of 24 miles. The wind was light, a bare seven knots, in which *Sceptre*'s soft bow was believed to be an advantage. This very rounded bow was David Boyd's advanced design which had shown up best in the tank tests. It was certainly unconventional and when

the Americans saw it they soon summed up the position, namely that Boyd was either very right or very wrong. What everyone knew was that the first mile or so would show beyond doubt which of the two, Olin Stevens or David Boyd, was right.

Both yachts came up to the starting line dead on and began the windward beat followed by no less than 1000 spectator craft, and among the personalities present was General Eisenhower, the President. Within minutes *Columbia* began to draw ahead and people waited anxiously to see *Sceptre* settle down and possibly sail through *Columbia*'s lee, but the unbelievable happened, and *Sceptre* never got going. There had been quite a breeze the day before and the sea had not quite died down. *Sceptre* was seen to be pitching rather like a hobby-horse and in the light wind doing worse than *Easterner* would have done, the least impressive of all the potential defenders.

There was nothing Mann could do. In fact, throughout the series he and his crew could hardly be faulted. By the outer mark, which *Sceptre* reached 7 minutes and 38 seconds after *Columbia*, they knew they had only one card left to play. This was the big herbulot spinnaker. As soon as this sail was set the gap began to close, hopes began to run high, and at the inner mark the difference in times was only 2 minutes 20 seconds. Unfortunately, to the disappointment of defenders as well as challengers, this new look was not to last. The wind now changed direction a couple of points making the final two legs both close reaches. *Columbia* went away with ease and, at the outer mark the second time, was 8 minutes 15 seconds ahead. Statisticians noted that in these conditions in the defender eliminator trials there was not more than one minute's difference between the yachts on such a leg. On the home run *Sceptre* cut the time by a trifle but still lost by 7 minutes 44 seconds.

It was a disaster. There was still one remote hope left. When the wind really blew *Sceptre* might show some more life. This consideration had been a special point in the examination of the hulls at the Saunders Roe tank, and *Sceptre*'s hull had come out best in the strong-wind conditions.

The next race was started in light airs shifting from one point on the compass to another. Mann showed the better judgement, so that with a little luck in his favour too, as to the quarter from which the next puff actually came, he reached the first mark of the triangular course 1 minute 45 seconds ahead. The spectator fleet gave him all they had on their horns and rattlers. This was in fact the only mark in the whole series when *Sceptre* was in the lead. Approaching the second mark *Columbia* had dropped to leeward a little further than *Sceptre* and the spectator fleet almost crowded round to give the challenger another terrific round of horns and rattlers, when the breeze suddenly strengthened and settled at about ten knots. To the astonishment of everyone *Columbia* just sailed right through *Sceptre*'s lee, a bare three lengths away, and rounded the mark 45 seconds ahead. The last leg now developed into a dead beat but time had run out and the race was abandoned, not before *Columbia* had walked away to a lead of over a mile. Graham Mann rightly asked for a lay day during which he could whistle for a really good blow.

On Wednesday 24 September the yachts raced over the triangular course again. Conditions were good with a 12-knot breeze. Graham Mann won the start hands down, and should have been able to take every advantage of it, but *Columbia* was so far superior when legging to windward that she sailed right through the challenger's weather, reaching the first mark 3 minutes 3 seconds ahead. On the second leg, where spinnakers counted and *Sceptre* by precept should have cut the lead, she unaccountably dropped further back and trailed by 8 minutes 45 seconds. The final leg only enlarged the gap, *Columbia* winning by 11 minutes 27 seconds. It was understandable that at this stage some gloom settled over the challenger's crew.

Next day the wind blew at 22 knots and rapidly dispersed the gloom in the *Sceptre* team. Their supporters in the spectator fleet took new heart too. Once again Graham Mann made a good start — some called it spectacular — but, sadly, in a very short time the defender was out ahead. In this strong breeze it was seen that *Sceptre* not only heeled more than *Columbia* but could not point so well. Graham Mann had a hopeless task. Twice round the outer mark and back again became a procession and in this race where *Sceptre* might have been expected to show some form she lost by 8 minutes 20 seconds.

The fourth race, sailed on Friday 26th, was remarkable only for the difficulties which Graham Mann and his crew overcame. Some skippers might have given up, particularly as there was no hope of winning the race, but not so Mann and his crew. As ever *Columbia* sailed away into the lead to such a distance that Cunningham had no idea what was going on in *Sceptre*. First a jib sheet fouled a cleat preventing the preparation of the spinnaker. Then, soon after this had been cleared and the Herbulot had been set the spinnaker guy parted and another had to be rove.

This was enough for one day but the bad luck had not yet run out. To the dismay of the crew the mainsail aluminium boom broke just forward of the kicking strap. The cause of this was that when resetting the spinnaker sheet it lifted the boom against the downward pull of the kicking strap and the boom snapped completely except for the steel sailtrack. Mann and his crew got to work immediately and 'fished' the boom, on one side with the boom crutch and on the other with the broken spinnaker boom. This was a first-class job well rewarded, as *Sceptre* dropped no more than 40 seconds on the leg and actually gained 1 minute 30 seconds on the final leg — a magnificent example of never giving up.

Naturally the question is asked, 'where did all this go wrong?' The answer appears to lie in the tank tests. No one is disputing the care and accuracy of the Saunders Roe testing, but there were serious limitations in the simulated conditions which led the experts at Saunders Roe, the syndicate and the designers astray. With a hull not in the same class as *Columbia*'s, and good sails, but not as good as the Americans', even a helmsman and crew equal to any American counterpart cannot produce

miracles. On reflection one wonders whether four top British yacht designers producing eight designs between them could possibly have designed seven yachts which in practice would have been slower than *Sceptre*. Even so, to match a proven defender of the Cup there has to be match practice with at least one or two top 12-metre yachts, and longer time for sail-adjusting, before a challenge can hope to succeed.

But whatever the critics may say the *Sceptre* story cannot be allowed to end on a note of utter despondency. In spite of all the disappointment the reception which *Sceptre* received at the finishing line at the end of the last race was tremendous. *Columbia*'s crew gave three cheers amid hooting and gunfire from the spectator fleet. Perhaps the action which counted most to Graham Mann and his crew was a signal sent by Commodore J. Burr Bartram of the New York Yacht Club. He quoted a signal from British naval history. It was sent by St Vincent to Nelson after the latter had failed to capture Tenneriffe: 'To mortals it is not given to command success, but you and your gallant companions have done more, you have deserved success.'

CHAPTER 10

Australian Challenge

Opinion was divided as to whether the tribulations of the *Sceptre* challenge would drown enthusiasm or encourage others to try and make amends. To the surprise of many the latter was the case. In England a syndicate bought *Sceptre* with the avowed intention of using her as a trial horse against another new yacht. Yet another syndicate, this time under Lord Craigmyle, came into the open, calling themselves the Red Duster Syndicate, because most members were prominent personalities in the shipping industry. They purchased the old 12-metre *Norsaga* as a start. But these moves towards another challenge from England were overtaken, rather out of the blue, by a challenge from Australia. It was sent by the Royal Sydney Yacht Squadron in the spring of 1960 on behalf of two brothers, F. and J. Livingstone, for a match in 1962.

Before this challenge was made some sound thinking had been going on in order to prevent another costly series producing no worthwhile racing. Sir Frank Packer, Managing Director of the Australian Consolidated Press, had chartered *Vim* for four years. This timely action allayed all fears, as it was clear that if the new 12-metre did not beat *Vim* the challenge would be withdrawn. Conversely if she even did as well as *Vim* in trials then the New York Yacht Club would have to look out.

Yachting in Australia is of a high standard, and Alan Payne, the designer of the challenger, not only had *Vim* to go by but was allowed to do tank tests in the Stevens tank at Hoboken, New Jersey. The yacht was built at Ryde, New South Wales, in the yard of Lars Halvorsen. She was named *Gretel* after Lady Packer. The De Havilland Aircraft Company sent out a 90-foot aluminium mast and the Sydney sailmakers Pearce and Cole ordered yards of dacron from the United States.

In March 1962 *Gretel*, equipped with everything which yachting enthusiasts down under could provide, started her working-up at Sydney against *Vim*. Rather naturally at the beginning there were troubles in the challenger, but as time went on it began to dawn on all close to the 'action' that she was getting a definite ascendancy over the trial horse.

The New York Yacht Club soon got to hear of all this and a new 12-metre was built at Boston, designed by F. Hood for a syndicate under E. Ross Anderson. She was named *Nefertiti*. During August 1962 the Americans held their selection trials. *Easterner* came on the scene once again and both *Columbia* and *Weatherly* were there. *Nefertiti*'s chief rival was *Weatherly*, which had been slightly altered as a result of massive racing experience and in the hands of the brilliant Mosbacher looked very good indeed.

In the early races *Nefertiti* came out well. *Easterner*, still very much a family affair, was rather easily beaten all round and in time *Columbia*, without her original crew, had to bow to *Weatherly*. Finally Mosbacher brought *Weatherly* home in front of *Nefertiti* in three consecutive races and this clinched the matter.

When the two yachts, *Weatherly* and *Gretel*, were seen together early in September the punters were at a loss as both yachts looked extremely similar in almost every detail.

The first race took place on 15 September. President John F. Kennedy was there in a destroyer together with the largest-ever spectator fleet, augmented by aircraft overhead and a large force of coastguard cutters clearing the course. Mosbacher's rival was Alexander Sturrock, a man

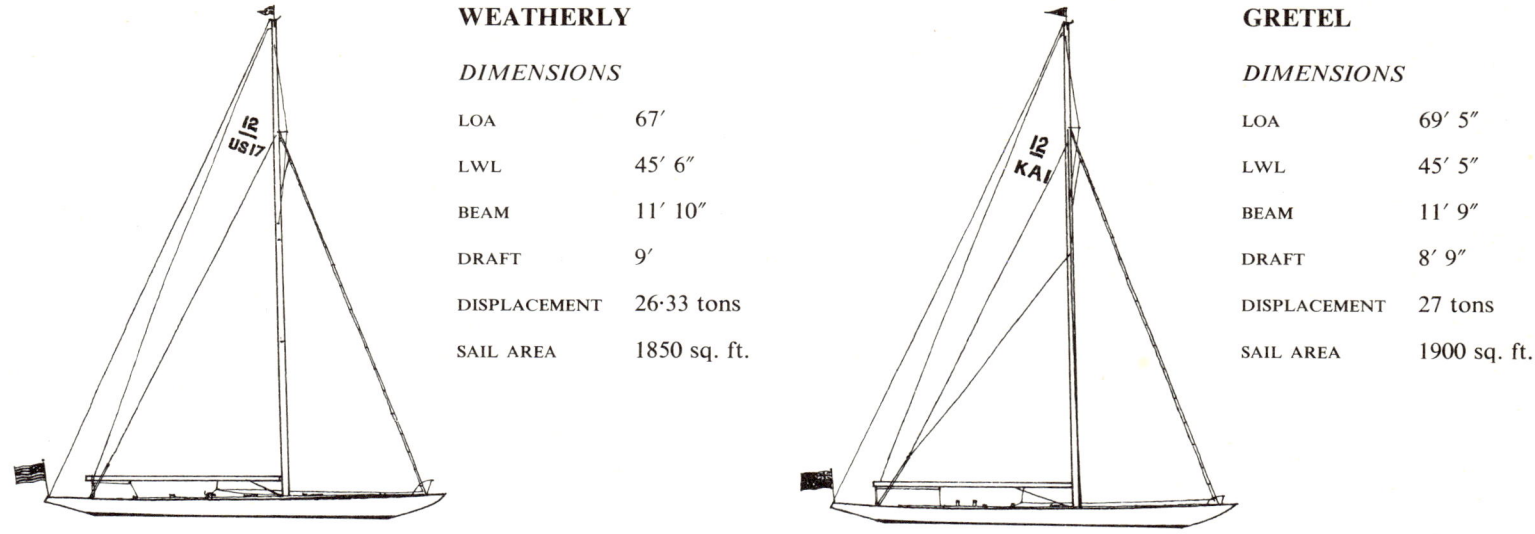

	WEATHERLY			GRETEL	
	DIMENSIONS			**DIMENSIONS**	
	LOA	67′		LOA	69′ 5″
	LWL	45′ 6″		LWL	45′ 5″
	BEAM	11′ 10″		BEAM	11′ 9″
	DRAFT	9′		DRAFT	8′ 9″
	DISPLACEMENT	26·33 tons		DISPLACEMENT	27 tons
	SAIL AREA	1850 sq. ft.		SAIL AREA	1900 sq. ft.

SERIES	DATE	NAME (winners name first)	COURSE	ELAPSED TIME	CORRECTED TIME	WINS BY	REMARKS
18th	September 15 1962	*WEATHERLY* *GRETEL*	6 miles to windward and return Twice round *24 miles*	3.13.57 3.17.43	12-metre sailed level	3m 46s	
18th	September 18 1962	*GRETEL* *WEATHERLY*	Triangular *24 miles*	2.46.48 2.47.45		0m 57s	
18th	September 20 1962	*WEATHERLY* *GRETEL*	6 miles to windward and return Twice round *24 miles*	4.21.16 4.29.56		8m 40s	
18th	September 22 1962	*WEATHERLY* *GRETEL*	Triangular *24 miles*	3.22.28 3.22.54		0m 26s	
18th	September 25 1962	*WEATHERLY* *GRETEL*	6 miles to windward and return Twice round *24 miles*	3.16.17 3.19.57		3m 40s	

every bit worthy of his position. In their first encounter Mosbacher got just the better of the start and then took *Weatherley* faster and pointing higher than *Gretel*. As ever it was the out-and-back course for the first contest, and at the outer mark the first time round *Weatherly* was just over a minute and a half ahead. Sail-shifting and spinnaker drill in both yachts were excellent, *Gretel* being perhaps slightly the better, but in spite of this 'edge' Mosbacher brought *Weatherly* home the winner by 3 minutes 46 seconds. This was rather more than most people had expected and for a few hours there was fear in many minds that this could be a repetition of the *Sceptre* series.

The second race was over the triangular course and was sailed on 18 September in an 18-knot breeze, which sometimes gusted up to 25 knots. Sturrock got slightly the better of the start but a little to the dismay of some experienced yachtsmen Mosbacher sailed through *Gretel*'s lee and placed herself some five lengths ahead. Sturrock immediately started a tacking duel which the Australians won, as after some ten tacks Mosbacher found his lead was dwindling, so set course for the first mark without covering and there was little in it when both yachts rounded the buoy.

The next leg needed genoas and the second mark was reached with *Weatherly* a bare 14 seconds in the lead. The final leg was a run, and here not only was *Gretel*'s spinnaker drill supreme, but *Weatherly* broke her spinnaker boom. *Gretel* romped away and to the tumultuous sounds of ships' sirens and gunfire she crossed the line the winner by 47 seconds. This had not happened since Sir Thomas Sopwith's challenge in 1934. Sturrock asked for a lay day to cool his brow.

The 20th September turned out to be a day of light winds more favourable to *Weatherly* than to *Gretel*, and although Sturrock made the better start he also made some mistakes. Firstly he overdid a tack and lost the initiative and later he kept too close to the spectator fleet, which gave him less steady winds than if he had given them a wider berth. The result was a great disappointment as he lost by the large margin of 8 minutes 40 seconds.

Sturrock immediately claimed another lay day in the hope that the wind might freshen in the next forty-eight hours. Unfortunately this was not to be, but *Gretel*'s helmsman and crew had learnt their lesson well in the third race and set about their task in light airs of 2 to 4 knots like hardened campaigners of the Newport roads. The result was a magnificent race round the triangular course with barely a boat's length between the yachts

all the way. Somehow Mosbacher managed to keep *Weatherly* just ahead at the vital moment and as the yachts came up to the finishing line he scraped home by 26 seconds after 24 miles of racing. It meant that the Cup stayed in America.

This fine race was all that the spectator fleet needed to keep them happy and, in spite of the final result having been settled, the Australians felt they had done a good job and came out for the last race full of spirit and determined to make it 3–2. It was the out-and-back course which always seemed to have an unseen helping hand for the defenders and, in spite of all that Sturrock could do, Mosbacher appeared to have little difficulty in winning by 3 minutes 40 seconds.

The press were full of praise for the Australians. All voted *Gretel*'s crew better than *Weatherly*'s and most put forward the view that had there been more racing in 20-knot winds *Gretel* would have won. All in all it was a very worthwhile challenge and a great encouragement to all bent on 'having a go'.

There followed two challenges which kept the interest alive but in themselves were not dramatic in comparison to most others. The first was made by the Royal Thames Yacht Club on behalf of Mr Anthony Boyden for races in 1964. The yacht, named *Sovereign*, was built to the design of David Boyd. Peter Scott, after much hard thinking because of his inexperience in this type of racing, accepted to take the helm. *Sovereign* lacked a trial horse, but this serious situation was overcome by the Livingstone Brothers who demonstrated Australian generosity and enthusiasm to the full by providing a similar yacht, *Kurrewa V*, to do the job, on the understanding that if she proved to be the better yacht in the trials she would have the honour of being the challenger.

Across the Atlantic the Americans had two particularly good yachts, *American Eagle* and *Constellation*. The latter, under the skilled helmsmanship of Bob Bavier, was selected to defend.

Sovereign showed up slightly better than *Kurrewa V* and was confirmed as challenger. Unfortunately, in spite of *Sovereign*'s crew being a match for *Constellation*'s, she was beaten all too easily in four races. Olin Stevens, Hood sails, and American expertise had been overwhelming.

The second challenge came from Australia. The America's Cup Challenge Syndicate of Petersville, Clayton, Victoria, challenged on behalf of the head of the syndicate, Mr E. Christenson, for races in 1967. The yacht was named *Dame Pattie*, and was built by W. H. Barrett of Sydney to the design of Warwick Hood.

The opposition was as strong as ever. Sparkman and Stevens designed *Intrepid* to defend. Four races in all were sailed and *Intrepid* won them all without being seriously challenged. Once again the Americans had the better boat and the better sails, but it was a worthwhile challenge as it emphasised to the Australians how much more they needed to do to win.

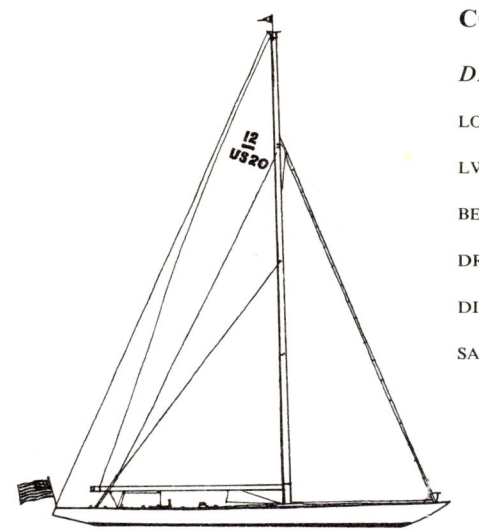

CONSTELLATION

DIMENSIONS

LOA	68′ 5″
LWL	46′
BEAM	11′ 11″
DRAFT	8′ 11″
DISPLACEMENT	26·07 tons
SAIL AREA	1818 sq. ft.

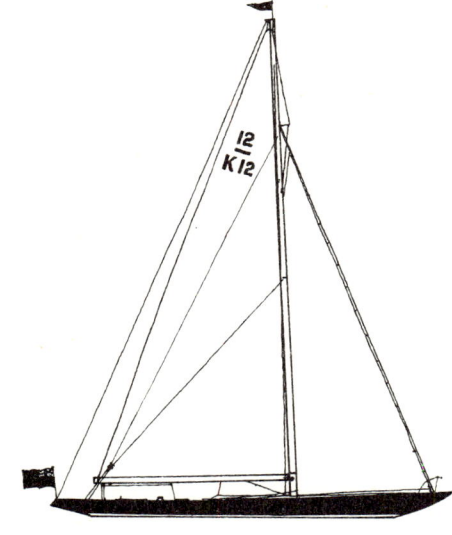

SOVEREIGN

DIMENSIONS

LOA	69′ 2″
LWL	45′ 8″
BEAM	12′ 6″
DRAFT	8′ 9″
DISPLACEMENT	27·67 tons
SAIL AREA	1860 sq. ft.

SERIES	DATE	NAME (winners name first)	COURSE	ELAPSED TIME	CORRECTED TIME	WINS BY	REMARKS
19th	September 15 1964	CONSTELLATION SOVEREIGN	Olympic Course 24.3 miles	3.30.41 3.36.15	12-metre sailed level	5m 34s	
19th	September 18 1964	CONSTELLATION SOVEREIGN	Olympic Course 24.3 miles	3.46.48 4.07.12		20m 24s	
19th	September 19 1964	CONSTELLATION SOVEREIGN	Olympic Course 24.3 miles	3.38.07 3.44.40		6m 33s	
19th	September 21 1964	CONSTELLATION SOVEREIGN	Olympic Course 24.3 miles	4.12.27 4.28.07		15m 40s	

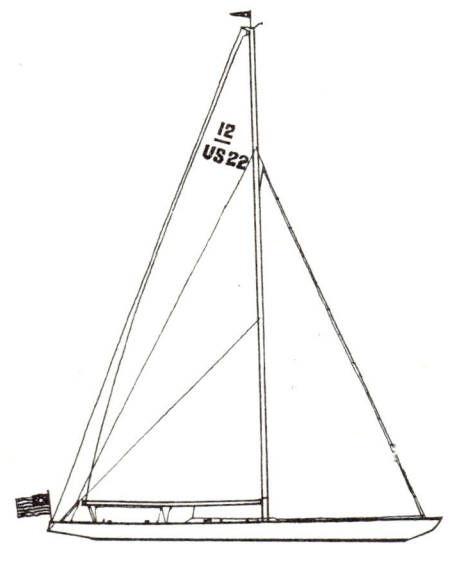

INTREPID

DIMENSIONS

LOA	63′ 3″
LWL	44′ 9″
BEAM	12′ 10″
DRAFT	8′ 11″
DISPLACEMENT	25 tons
SAIL AREA	N.K.

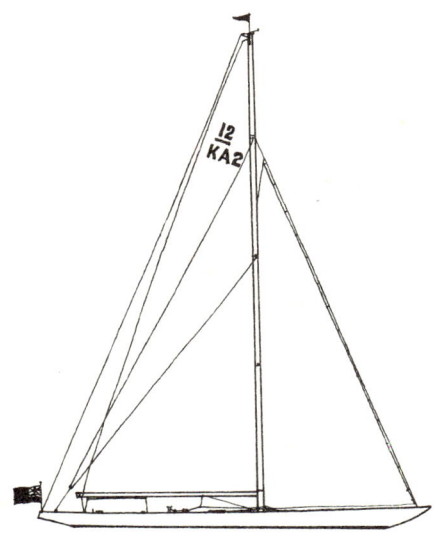

DAME PATTIE

DIMENSIONS

LOA	65′ 6″
LWL	46′ 11″
BEAM	11′ 11″
DRAFT	9′ 1″
DISPLACEMENT	26·78 tons
SAIL AREA	1795 sq. ft.

SERIES	DATE	NAME (winners name first)	COURSE	ELAPSED TIME	CORRECTED TIME	WINS BY	REMARKS
20th	September 12 1967	INTREPID DAME PATTIE	Olympic Course 24.3 miles	3.25.03 3.31.01	12-metre sailed level	6m 57s	
20th	September 13 1967	INTREPID DAME PATTIE	Olympic Course 24.3 miles	3.29.21 3.32.57		3m 36s	
20th	September 14 1967	INTREPID DAME PATTIE	Olympic Course 24.3 miles	3.20.14 3.24.55		4m 41s	
20th	September 18 1967	INTREPID DAME PATTIE	Olympic Course 24.3 miles	3.27.39 3.31.14		3m 35s	

CHAPTER 11

The Centenary Races

Yachtsmen all over the world now looked ahead to the centenary year 1970. It seemed that this anniversary would set a pattern for many years to come. Either it would be hopelessly one-sided and thereby the contest would virtually cease to exist or from some quarter there would be a revival of skill in design and helmsmanship which would put new life into this greatest of all yachting competitions. Time would show.

It was therefore a source of the greatest satisfaction to all lovers of this sport when three challenges for the centenary year were made. Sir Frank Packer challenged through the Royal Sydney Yacht Squadron, followed by a newcomer, Baron Marcel Bich, who announced his wish to compete through the 'Association Française Pour La Coupe America', and to the delight of all English yachtsmen, Erik Maxwell, the present owner of *Sceptre*, issued his challenge through the Royal Dorset Yacht Club. Unhappily the English challenge had to be withdrawn at an early stage when Maxwell was unable to raise the necessary money, leaving the honours to Australia and France.

In Australia most yachtsmen prefer to forget the 1967 *Dame Pattie* series. In the first race against *Intrepid*, helmed by Bus Mosbacher, it was clear that the defenders had much the best boat and the Australian crew found it difficult to sustain the enthusiasm vital to a challenging team, a factor unrepresentative of Australians. Apart therefore from the incentive to try and win in the centenary year there was the urge to wipe out the memory of 1967. Having stood down in that year, Sir Frank Packer now embarked on his second attempt, naming his yacht *Gretel II*, to try his skill.

Training started in 1968. Apart from a six weeks' break in the winter, two 12-metre yachts, one *Vim*, originally chartered and then bought, and the other the first *Gretel*, raced against each other every weekend until the second *Gretel* was ready. These trials were used to evaluate potential skippers and principal crewmen. Alan Payne, the prospective designer of the new yacht, watched every race and in his own words 'learnt a lot'.

Gretel II was built by Bill Barnett at Milson's Point, Sydney. She was launched in November 1969 and was ready for sailing in February 1970. The main innovations were a bigger sail fore triangle and new ideas in the deck layout, of which a mock-up had been built so that the two trial crews could make suggestions and comments. Trial horses were *Gretel I* and *Dame Pattie*, the latter brought out of retirement.

The trials were very disappointing. Not only did the new yacht show up badly against her ten-year old namesake, but *Dame Pattie*, so decisively beaten by *Intrepid* in 1967, beat both the *Gretels* with some ease. There were many troubles. The yacht seemed to be out of balance so the mast was moved two feet forward. This done the size of the rudder was doubled.

But the consensus of opinion was directed more to the sails and rigging, the former having to be extensively recut. Besides all this, a view repeatedly expressed over the last hundred years was again emphasised in Australia, namely that the race would not be won on the drawing boards alone but by the helmsman, the crew, the sailmaker, the sailcloth manufacturer, the designer, the boat builder and the team co-ordinator. Some said 'in that order' and probably they were not far wrong.

Still far from fully worked-up, *Gretel II* arrived in Boston on 1 August

and was then towed to Newport, Rhode Island, for fitting out. There she was met by Alan Payne, Jim Hardy, the skipper who had come out best in all those early months of racing, and Martin Visser, relief to Hardy. No trial horse was brought to Newport and as a lighter mast was shipped shortly after arrival Australia's challenger at that time remained very much an unknown quantity.

Naturally the Australian plans to bring a worthwhile challenger to Newport were followed all over the world with the greatest interest, but what made the preliminaries to the centenary series so fascinating was the entry of France into the contest. Never before had that country made a challenge, so the preparations in France were followed as closely as possible, an exercise made specially difficult as the *France* was built in great secrecy. Lack of experience seemed to be one of the disadvantages with which Baron Bich would have to contend but he spent money on an America's Cup scale. Not only did he buy as many modern 12-metre yachts as were available for sale, including England's *Sovereign* and *Kurrewa V* and America's *Constellation*, but having been prevented by the New York Yacht Club from buying *Intrepid* he ordered a new yacht from America which was built by Britton Chance, the young 5.5-metre architect, and named *Chancegger* to serve as an additional trial horse against the design produced for him by André Mauric.

Traditionally the America's Cup race produces many remarkable characters who enliven the contest and add to its fascination. The arrival of Baron Bich on the scene carried on that tradition. It appears that he had been looking for some challenge to enrich his life, not with money-making in mind — he had all he needed through his Bic ball-point pens — but to spend his money on some great achievement. He settled on the America's Cup.

For two years his fleet of four 12-metre yachts raced in the Mediterranean and then he set about building his challenger 3000 feet up in the Jura Mountains, at Pontarlier, not far from the Swiss border.

In June the Baron arrived in Newport where he spread himself across the harbour at the most expensive moorings, accommodating a 70-foot ex-R.A.F. air-sea rescue launch, two 30-foot fibreglass tenders and three 12-metre yachts. Ashore he took over a mansion called the Miramar, normally a girls school, in order to house his wife, nine children, thirty-three yachtsmen, five carpenters and sailmakers, four technicians, two clerks, two divers and a *maitre d'hôtel*, a masseuse, two pastry cooks and a *cordon bleu* chef. On arrival he said that this was a long-term scheme. He was determined to succeed where British, Australians, Irish and Canadians had all failed. If he lost this time he intended to come back time and time again.

The Americans for their part had never taken a challenge lightly and set about the centenary preliminaries in the usual very thorough fashion. There were two series of trials, the first of which took place in July. The four yachts competing were *Weatherly*, the 1962 winner against *Gretel I*, now skippered by the 65-year-old George Hinman, *Heritage*, designed and owned and skippered by Charley Morgan from Florida, the first boat to come from the south in America's Cup history, *Intrepid*, the winner of the 1967 series against *Dame Pattie* now redesigned by Britton Chance and skippered by Bill Ficker, and *Valiant*, a new Olin Stevens boat owned by a syndicate and skippered by Bob McCullough.

The result of the first trials showed that *Intrepid* looked better than *Valiant*, the then favourite. *Heritage* did well enough on one occasion by beating *Valiant* only to be beaten by *Weatherly* two days later. The second and final eliminating trials took place in August when, as expected, *Weatherly* was soon eliminated. *Heritage* was the next to be dropped, in many respects rather sadly because Charley Morgan had set his heart on being 'in' on this contest. He had a beautiful yacht and had worked himself to the bone. Some said he lost through his own physical exhaustion. The final choice between *Valiant* and *Intrepid* took some time to decide. Both helmsmen, who had done none too well in previous years when sailing in eliminating trials, improved with every hour but when *Intrepid* won five consecutive races she was named to defend the Cup.

On Friday 21 August the spectator fleet set out to sea to watch the first of seven races between *Gretel II* and *France*. So far as the experts could tell this might be quite a contest running the whole seven races. Sir Frank Packer had put all the sailing knowledge he could muster in Australia into his *Gretel II* and the Baron Bich had invested over a million pounds in his preparations. The only sure thing which spectators knew was that, in the early days after the arrival of *France* in Newport Roads, *Constellation* had been beating *France* quite easily. Something which was not certain was whether the choice of Novarrez as skipper for the first race might have been bettered. He was named only the day before and during the working-up at least two good French helmsmen had been either dismissed by the Baron or had resigned from the team. In fact the French had been making the news and their spectacular approach to this serious business had been highlighted when *France* put to sea on 14 July, Bastille Day, and hoisted a huge spinnaker bearing the insignia of the Province of Paris. So the scene was set for the first eliminating race to choose a challenger from the two different countries, a circumstance entirely new to America's Cup contests. To referee the race and judge any protest the International Yacht Racing Union had provided a committee of impartial and experienced yachtsmen.

The first race was sailed in light and uncertain winds which the Swiss skipper Louis Novarrez handled with great skill and led Jim Hardy in *Gretel II* at every mark with a clear margin until the fifth. Here Novarrez took *France* round in a tight turn while Hardy ran wide keeping his sails well filled. This not only paid dividends but drew the luck, as *France* momentarily lost the wind at the same time as *Gretel* ran into a steady patch. Onlookers who had confidently credited *France* with the first win were astounded to see *Gretel* sail away from her rival and win by over six minutes.

Understandably the French were equally dumbfounded and felt they had been done out of a win by sheer hard luck. With this most Australians agreed, including Jim Hardy who openly acknowledged that Novarrez had outsailed him over all but the last leg of the course. To the yachting world *Gretel II* and *France* had achieved a major breakthrough in interest and skill, a factor which to many overrode all other considerations.

The Baron took a different view and blamed his skipper for a tactical error. For this he relieved him of the helm and appointed Pierre Delfour whom he had fired a fortnight earlier but who had remained in Newport

and was ready to accept the offer. This was not the only change, as a new crew was chosen and following an eight-hour sail *France*'s headstay was eased and her mast slightly raked. This shocked all who had experience of this sort of racing, as to make experiments when in full pursuit of the target is almost unthinkable.

The second race was a thriller. The two yachts were never very far apart and sometimes changed places, *Gretel* appearing not to be so good as *France*. However once again the Australian yacht came from behind and this time won by one minute and thirty-two seconds. Those who saw the blue-hulled *France* and the white-hulled *Gretel* fight it out over 24.3 miles, with seldom more than 200 yards between them and the boats sometimes almost touching, had a thrilling day. Notably *France* tacked 17 times in 20 minutes at one stage and showed that crew for crew there was nothing much between them.

It would have been fairer if *France* had come in first on one of those races. Spectators agreed that here was racing worthy of America's Cup challengers and that, whatever else happened, the years of disappointment when *Sceptre*, *Soveriegn* and *Dame Pattie* failed badly could be thankfully forgotten.

In the face of two defeats the Baron recalled Novarrez and changed three of the crew. Opinion was divided on the merits of the 68-year old Swiss and the 34-year old Delfour, a skipper of international fame but in smaller yachts. As regards the yachts themselves it was noticed that Baron Bich's challenger appeared to be a little faster than *Gretel II* and certainly went to windward well, a key feature to winning an America's Cup series.

The third race was sailed in a fair wind, so there were no excuses and it was a true test of the yachts and their crews. In this the Australians came out top all along the course. *Gretel* was never behind and won by a comfortable margin of 2 minutes 24 seconds. It was clear that the Baron would do something drastic for the fourth race which could be the last for *France*. His answer to the problem was to announce that he would sail the yacht himself taking with him the round-the-world yachtsman Eric Tabarly. He also changed masts with his other 12-metre *Chancegger*. Not surprisingly Delfour refused to come along too.

The final race, sailed on 28 August, was a fiasco. There were only light airs and this always makes the chances of a start on the very second of the gun more difficult. In this case *France* found herself a hundred yards astern of *Gretel II* when the gun went. The rest of the race was sailed in fog and whereas *Gretel II* struck every mark exactly right ahead, *France* became hopelessly lost and never found the finishing line. Thus in four straight races the French challenge, on which so much money had been expended and which represented some five years planning, was ruled out.

It was natural that Baron Bich should express his disappointment and at a press conference he complained that to race in such conditions was dangerous and quoted the international rule that a boat should be able to stop in half its visibility. In answer to this Commodore Frederick Horn, of Norway, spoke out on behalf of himself and Dr Beppe Croce and Mr Ernst Oscar Ahlers, of the America's Cup International Race Committee, insisting that nothing in the rules said anything about fog, rain or loss of wind or any other reason for calling off the race once it had started, other

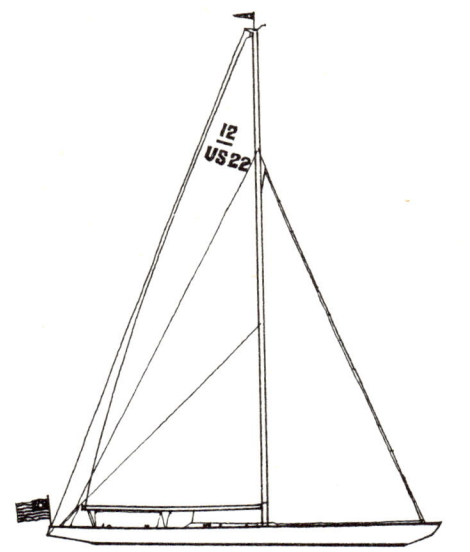

INTREPID

DIMENSIONS

LOA	64' 6"
LWL	46'
BEAM	12' 10"
DRAFT	9'
DISPLACEMENT	N.K.
SAIL AREA	N.K.

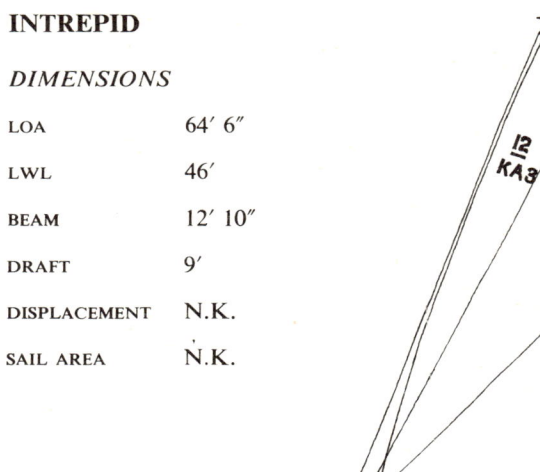

GRETEL II

DIMENSIONS

LOA	62'
LWL	N.K.
BEAM	12' 3"
DRAFT	9' 6"
DISPLACEMENT	30 tons
SAIL AREA	N.K.

SERIES	DATE	NAME (winners name first)	COURSE	ELAPSED TIME	CORRECTED TIME	WINS BY	REMARKS
21st	September 15 1970	*INTREPID* *GRETEL II*	Olympic Course *24.3 miles*	3.26.03 3.31.55	12-metre sailed level	5m 52s	
21st	September 20 1970	*GRETEL II* *INTREPID*	Olympic Course *24.3 miles*	4.37.03 4.38.10		1m 07s	*GRETEL II* *disqualified*
21st	September 22 1970	*INTREPID* *GRETEL II*	Olympic Course *24.3 miles*	3.24.43 3.26.01		1m 18s	
21st	September 24 1970	*GRETEL II* *INTREPID*	Olympic Course *24.3 miles*	3.23.59 3.25.01		1m 02s	
21st	September 28 1970	*INTREPID* *GRETEL II*	·Olympic Course *24.3 miles*	4.29.03 4.30.47		1m 44s	

than the six-hour limit. 'It never entered our minds,' he said, 'to call off the race and with the coastguard boat following *France* and plotting her course I am sure they did not think it dangerous either.'

It could be said that *France* had been eliminated more by bad luck than by bad management in the first races but on the subject of this fourth, *Gretel*'s skipper, Hardy, let it be known that while *Gretel II* was building the question of navigating in fog was carefully considered. Bill Fesq, already nominated navigator, had asked for and been granted certain space in the yacht necessary for navigating in low visibility. Fesq did very well 'on the day' and it only goes to show yet again that to win the America's Cup every detail has to be considered a long time before the contest takes place. Those who take important positions in the crew must be very good at their job.

The intervening period between the end of the eliminating trials and the actual America's Cup races was made full use of by all concerned. The Baron Bich took the opportunity to reply to the criticisms of the International Committee who were so outspoken after his press conference. In a letter to the *New York Times* he said that Commodore Horn and his Race Committee had used the press to make public intemperate and libellous statements against his person instead of sticking to the facts of the case. He cited a *New York Times* reporter as saying that most observers agreed that the Committee, in the interest of public safety in the final race, should have notified the French yacht to stop racing. To the charge that his crew lacked navigational experience he reminded the public that he had entrusted the navigation to Eric Tabarly, the round-the-world yachtsman. Thankfully the Race Committee did not pursue this heated exchange but the fact did emerge that Dr Croce, by order of the Committee's Chairman, had sent a radio message to the tender *Cheetah*, instructing her to inform *France* that she was steering away from the finishing line.

Meanwhile Bich, true to an earlier agreement with the Australians, had provided *Gretel II* with much needed race practice and every day either *France* or *Chancegger* was out with the Australians to try and make up for their lack of hard sailing against a trial horse. In these exercises no set course was sailed but it became clear that *Gretel II* was definitely faster than either of the French yachts, so no one really questioned the Australians' right to the honour of being the challenger. *Intrepid*'s crew hardly needed any further work-up. They spent their time perfecting drill and trying out yet more sails. They took advantage

too of getting in some well earned rest.

So on the great day, 15 September, the spectator fleet assembled with mixed feelings. They recalled that the last real contest had been sailed in 1962 when the first *Gretel* won one race. Statisticians noted that *Endeavour II* in 1937, *Sceptre* in 1958, *Sovereign* in 1964 and *Dame Pattie* in 1967, had all been beaten by four races to nil. Only *Shamrock IV* in 1920 and the first *Endeavour* in 1934, besides *Gretel II*'s predecessor, had given the Americans a run. So much for the record book, but conversation in the 1000 or more ships and yachts went further than this. People recalled the moment which some had witnessed when Jock Sturrock in *Gretel I* overtook the great Bus Mosbacher in *Weatherly*, and *Gretel II* had come from the same stable. Some talked of the latest New York Yacht Club rule which disallowed a challenger's sails to be made in America, and the immense research which had been done throughout Europe and in Australia to improve weave and to design sets of sails for all conditions. Above all every one hoped for a close contest and whether this would be the case or not would be made clear before the first leg of the 21st series had been sailed.

Apart from what was being said in the spectator fleet there were some further interesting reflections on this centenary contest. Any America's Cup contest is for many a thrill of a lifetime and particularly for the principals. In this case there were six very wealthy yachtsmen in the *Intrepid* syndicate pitted against one Australian yachtsman newspaper magnate. Win or lose their yachts would be worth very little and to convert them to ocean racers would run away with 100,000 dollars or more. Phil Ganes, the leading expert at Minneford Yacht Works in New York, where *Intrepid* was built, estimated the original boat cost 400,000 dollars. The sails were made at Hood's works at Marblehead, Massachusetts, and *Intrepid* would have had in her locker 2 or 3 mainsails at 5000 dollars each, 9 or 10 jibs at not less than 2000 dollars each and the same number of spinnakers at about the same price.

American comment summed all this up pretty shrewdly. One of *Intrepid*'s crew remarked, 'Everybody is mad in his own way. Putting money and time into an America's Cup challenge or defence is just another sort of madness'. Briggs Dalzel, one of the American syndicate, thought it 'great fun and I love it. Besides we are all pretty well off', while Bob Bavier, the successful helmsman against *Sovereign* in *Constellation* in 1967, came nearest to the mark when he said, 'They just happen to think the America's Cup is important'.

One technicality also reared its head before the yachts lined up for the start. Britton Chance had given *Intrepid* a new design for the rudder which he placed right aft and kept it in position by fairing strips. Sir Frank Packer protested that these strips increased the yacht's wetted surface, in other words its length, thereby giving her an advantage. As a result of this Mr William Strawbridge, Manager of *Intrepid*'s syndicate, said that the fairing strips would be changed but not taken off. Later David Thorpe, the experienced yachting reporter for the English *Daily Telegraph*, made these comments: '*Intrepid* is equivalent to say a 12¼-metre, which will always place the Australians at a disadvantage. This is because of the New York Yacht Club's ruling that her rudder could be hung behind the waterline end and then joined to the keel by fairing strips which effectively increases her underwater length from 47 feet to 48 feet 6 inches. That makes 0.1 knot of difference or say 1½ minutes in a 2½ hour race.' The fact is that this change in design exposed a loophole in the design conditions which was not revealed in *Intrepid* until she was seen docked shortly before the racing was due to begin. This important point has now been debated by the International Yacht Racing Union Technical Committee and the following is a summary of the protest and the action resulting from it:

Intrepid was altered to include a fairing between the after end of the keel and the leading edge of the rudder which was placed aft of the end of the waterline. Sir Frank Packer challenged this innovation on the grounds that it increased the waterline thereby increasing the speed of the yacht. The measurer of the New York Yacht Club, under whose rules the contest was being sailed, judged it to be within the rules.

Since then there has been much discussion on the question of fairings and on 10 November 1970 the International Yacht Racing Union Technical Committee, at their Annual Conference at the Royal Thames Yacht Club in London, amended sections of the 12-metre rules to clarify the measurement of waterline length, paying particular attention to the question of fairing strips.

These amended rules are under notice and will come into force for 12-metres in March 1972 with the intention of them being used in the next America's Cup contest.

The sketch below shows the general principle of fairings.

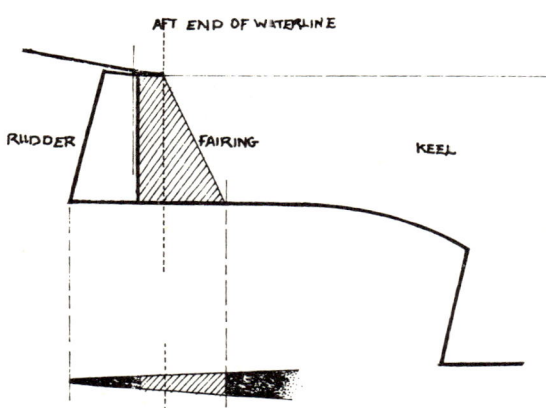

Fairings are not necessarily made of wood. In one instance the material used was a rubbery substance which gave way easily to water pressure and would bend in and out with the pressure of water passing over it.

All the races were sailed over the Olympic course of 24.3 miles consisting of six legs, first a beat to windward then two reaches to complete the triangle and then three legs to windward, leeward, windward. On the morning of 15 September the early mist gave way to rain with a brisk wind of 18 knots. The visibility was a good two miles. *Intrepid* won

the start gaining the weather position and footing better to windward and rounded the first mark 1 minute 3 seconds in the lead. When *Gretel II* rounded she had a really bad mix-up when setting her spinnaker which became twisted. For several minutes the crew tried to correct the twist but gave this up temporarily and set a second spinnaker. By the time the first had been hauled down and the second was drawing fully *Intrepid* had broken away to a winning lead. This she held easily because at the third mark, while changing the spinnaker for a genoa, one of *Gretel II*'s crew fell overboard. Hardy had to turn about to pick him up, not only for his own safety but because the rules state that a yacht must finish with the same number of crew as it had on board at the start. For the rest of the race the Australians held on all they could but had no hope of catching the defender which won by 5 minutes 52 seconds. Both yachts finished flying protest flags which concerned some of the manoeuvring before the start, but these protests were not allowed by the Committee so *Intrepid* was one up in the series. Commentators recalled the *Endeavour* incident in 1934 when 'a man fell overboard', but this was not truly the case as has been described earlier in this book. The man went overboard but held on to the halyard and was quickly pulled inboard, and this version of the incident has been authenticated by Sir Thomas Sopwith himself who, of course, was sailing *Endeavour* at the time. *Gretel* asked for a lay day so there was no action on the 16th.

When 17 September dawned there was hardly a breath of wind. Both yachts went out to the starting line but the race was cancelled after the crews and the spectator fleet had sunbathed for two hours. The race on the 18th was very frustrating for everybody. It was abandoned when the yachts were approaching the fourth mark. There had been a tight duel in dense fog and driving rain but practically no wind at all. When it was called off *Intrepid* had a lead of about six lengths.

The next race, on Sunday 20th, had not even begun before drama set in. While the wind was still very light and the Committee were holding on for a better breeze, Van Dyke, *Intrepid*'s tactician, was stung by a bee close to the ear and had to be winched off by a helicopter and taken to hospital. Hardly had this setback to the defender been dealt with when a coastguard cutter reported a Second World War floating mine among the spectator fleet. Naval ships were rushed to the position and pronounced it a disused fisherman's buoy, to the relief of all concerned not the least the Committee who were about to hoist the starting signal. It should be stated here that these gentlemen were in a ship named *Incredible*, and as the yachts came up to the starting line they were in a perfect position to see what might be termed a barging match, as *Gretel* under the helm of Martin Visser, her co-helmsman, had hung about near the line while *Intrepid* had stood off in order to make a perfectly timed flying start. Visser, seeing his rival bear down on him and the Committee boat, luffed to prevent this tactic and almost simultaneously the starting gun was fired. From this point the yachts were under racing rules and it was incumbent on *Gretel* not to carry the luff through the wind on to the opposite tack. This she did and also struck *Intrepid* abaft the mast. Thus *Intrepid* sailed through to a lead but, as soon as Hardy took over the helm in *Gretel* from Martin Visser, Bill Ficker, in *Intrepid*, was put to his most exacting test which he just managed to win until the last leg but one, which was a run. Here Hardy found the best spinnaker for the conditions and, as in the races against *France*, came through from behind and led at the last mark. All he had to do then was to cover every move of the defender on the windward beat to the finish. This he did very successfully and crossed the line 1 minute 8 seconds the winner. Here there was a repetition of the first *Gretel*'s challenge when she beat *Weatherly* in the second race and hopes were once more raised that *Gretel II* would not end the contest with a 1 - 4 defeat.

As the yachts crossed the line both were flying protest flags and the Committee announced that they would consider them on Monday. The members had before them two rules. One of these states that when approaching the starting line a leeward yacht may luff to windward to prevent the passage of a yacht on the windward side. However, after the starting gun has gone and before the line has been crossed, this tactic is not allowed. *Intrepid* protested under this rule. The other rule simply states that the overtaking yacht must keep clear of the yacht ahead. *Gretel* quoted this rule.

The Committee, who saw the incident most clearly from *Incredible* (it happened almost under their noses), ruled in favour of *Intrepid* and America were consequently two up. For their part the Australians were bitter and once again cries went up for an independent international committee and not surprisingly the word *Incredible* was much in evidence. The fact is, however, that *Gretel II* was absolutely wrong and it was a thousand pities that the New York Yacht Club found themselves forced to give their own boat the verdict. The last disqualification was when the Earl of Dunraven's *Valkyrie III* fouled the defender in 1895, with consequences which led to the Earl abandoning the final race and sailing for home. Thankfully, in spite of their disappointment and some hard words, the Australians increased their determination to win, comforting themselves that they had had the better of *Intrepid* over 24.3 miles.

It was thought that in the next race, on Tuesday 22nd, *Gretel* would keep clear of *Intrepid*, at least at the start, but this was not so at all. *Gretel* harried her rival all the time up to the starting gun but to no avail and Bill Ficker, full of confidence with two wins in the bag, outsailed Hardy. But it was close all the way, sometimes with only a few seconds in it when a mistake by either could have been fatal. This time neither made any mistake, there were no protests and in a wind rising to 17 knots *Intrepid* crossed the line 1 minute 18 seconds in the lead. Ficker immediately asked for a lay day and said it would be used to try out more sails. Having found a head sail which seemed to have evened out *Gretel's* slight advantage in footing to windward and also a spinnaker which seemed to match the one in *Gretel* which took her ahead in the second race, Ficker wanted to test a few more in his locker.

So the Americans had to win only one more race to retain the Cup and it looked to the experts as though 1934 was going to be repeated. Then, Sopwith had the faster yacht and lost. To many *Gretel II* was the fastest 12-metre afloat, but they still did not think she would win. American defensive tactics in every aspect of the game are so good that few people could see them losing now. But the Australians were not going to go out without a tough fight and the next race set all yachtsmen agog with excitement.

On Thursday 24 September the wind was blowing at 12 knots, strong enough to give *Intrepid* a fair chance of holding *Gretel* on the windward legs. Once again the race was a close one, almost neck and neck, and much of it dictated by slight changes in the direction of the wind with the yachts struggling to take advantage whenever the opportunity appeared. At the first mark *Intrepid* led by 29 seconds, but once again on the first spinnaker run *Gretel* closed the gap, though this time by only five seconds. The third and fourth legs were Ficker's. He disregarded his opponent and went for the wind shifts. This was a chancy business and sent the hearts of his supporters into their mouths. *Gretel's* first opportunity to keep the series open came at the fifth leg, which was the final run, but the unexpected happened and instead of gaining on *Intrepid* the defender's lead increased to 60 seconds. With the sixth and final leg, a beat, it appeared that the centenary challenge was over until an over-confident Bill Ficker, with the race in his pocket, failed to cover *Gretel*. Hardy did the only possible thing in his position and legged it to windward as hard as he could go. Then the luck turned in his favour. The next shift of wind found him in a position to reach for the line a bit off the wind and going fast. It was too late then for Ficker to cover and the Australians had won a race well and truly this time by 63 seconds bringing the score to 3–1.

For one reason and another the fifth race was not held until Monday 28th. Once again the wind was about 12 knots and the first leg was a real thriller. Hardy got slightly the better of the start but Ficker, by dint of really concentrated sailing, using his expert crew to help in every slight move or detail, managed to reach the first mark in the lead. From then, remembering how he had come to grief by not covering *Gretel* in the

previous race, he set about his business with a fierce determination to keep ahead at all costs.

This was the pattern of the race until the yachts came to what might be called *Gretel's* ground, namely the true run downwind, and in *Gretel's* favour by this time the wind had dropped to about 7 knots. So with the yachts only four lengths apart and the situation precisely what Sir Frank Packer's yacht had been designed for the scene was set for *Gretel's* final chance. Yet, as the yachts skimmed silently down that fifth leg *Intrepid* held her ground and at the final turn Bill Ficker had only to cover Hardy up the windward leg to retain the Cup. In the event the wind made a slight shift which favoured the leading boat and *Intrepid* sailed over the finishing line to win by 1 minute 44 seconds, and the Cup stayed in America.

For the next week yachting experts filled the sporting columns of the world's papers with their summaries of this memorable series. With all that they wrote and much that was said as well the conclusions seem to be these. *Gretel II* was the faster yacht and in 1970 could be said to be the fastest 12-metre in the world. That she did not win was due to two factors. The first was Sir Frank Packer's decision, as far back as 1968, that he would not proceed with this challenge if any other Australian syndicate also entered. Through this, *Gretel II* was deprived of the close match practice essential in the winning of an America's Cup series, and Jim Hardy's crew were not able to produce the expertise which all American crews develop before they do battle. The second factor was related to the first in that *Intrepid*, a redesigned yacht, beat *Valiant*, a new yacht, through superior helmsmanship and drill and learnt how to beat a potentially faster yacht. Thus when they met another faster yacht in the challenge series this was nothing new and they were confident as to how to go about it and win.

The story goes that on one occasion, when Bus Mosbacher, the well-known American helmsman, stood gazing at the America's Cup in its special place in the New York Yacht Club, he turned to the President and asked, 'What do you think we will put in its place if we lose?' The answer was short and to the point: 'The skull of the guy who lost it.'

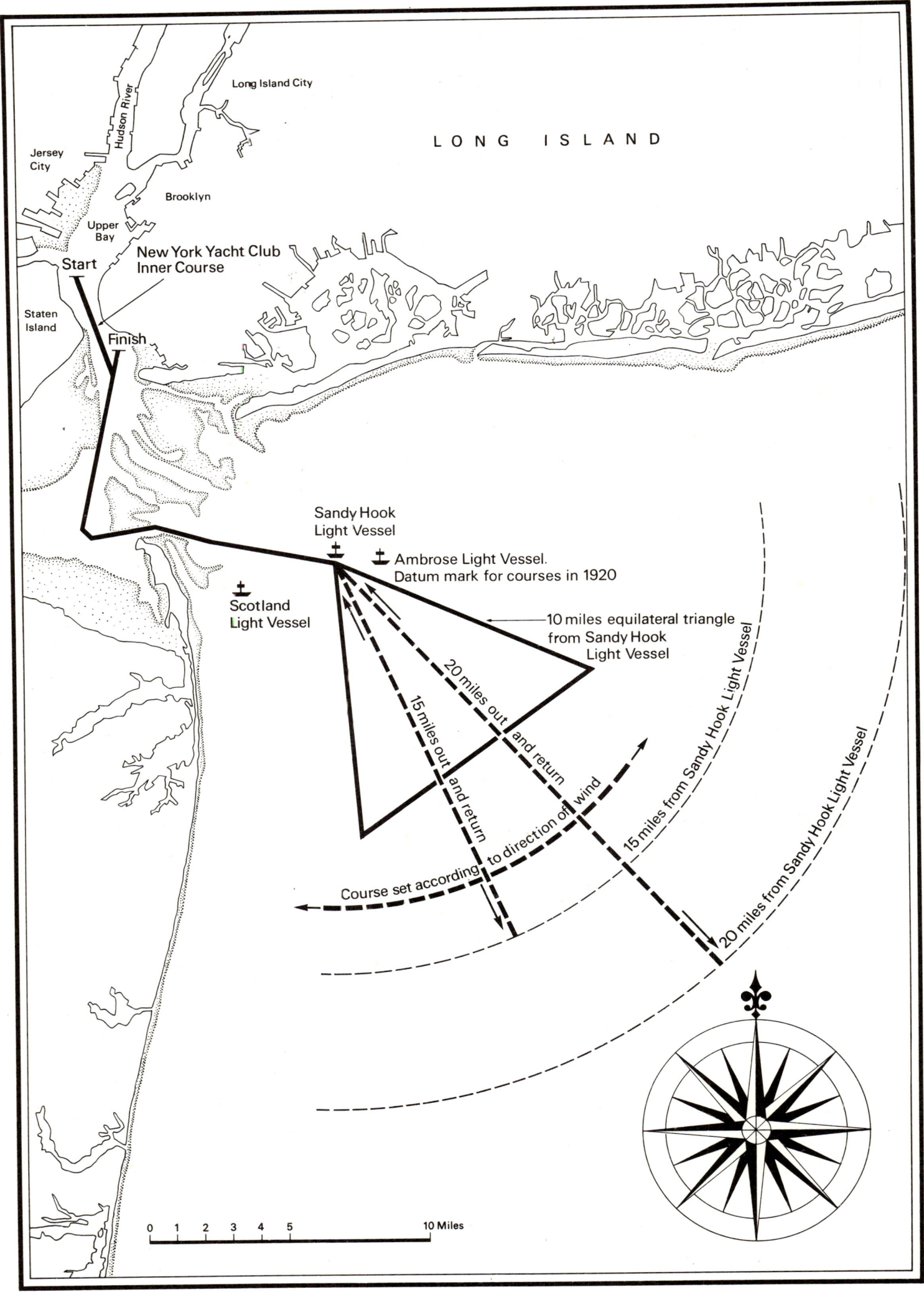

Long Island City

Hudson River

Jersey City

Brooklyn

LONG ISLAND

Upper Bay

Start

New York Yacht Club
Inner Course

Staten Island

Finish

Sandy Hook
Light Vessel

Ambrose Light Vessel.
Datum mark for courses in 1920

Scotland
Light Vessel

10 miles equilateral triangle
from Sandy Hook
Light Vessel

20 miles out and return

15 miles out and return

15 miles from Sandy Hook Light Vessel

20 miles from Sandy Hook Light Vessel

Course set according to direction of wind

0 1 2 3 4 5   10 Miles

**America's Cup Courses off New York
1870-1920**

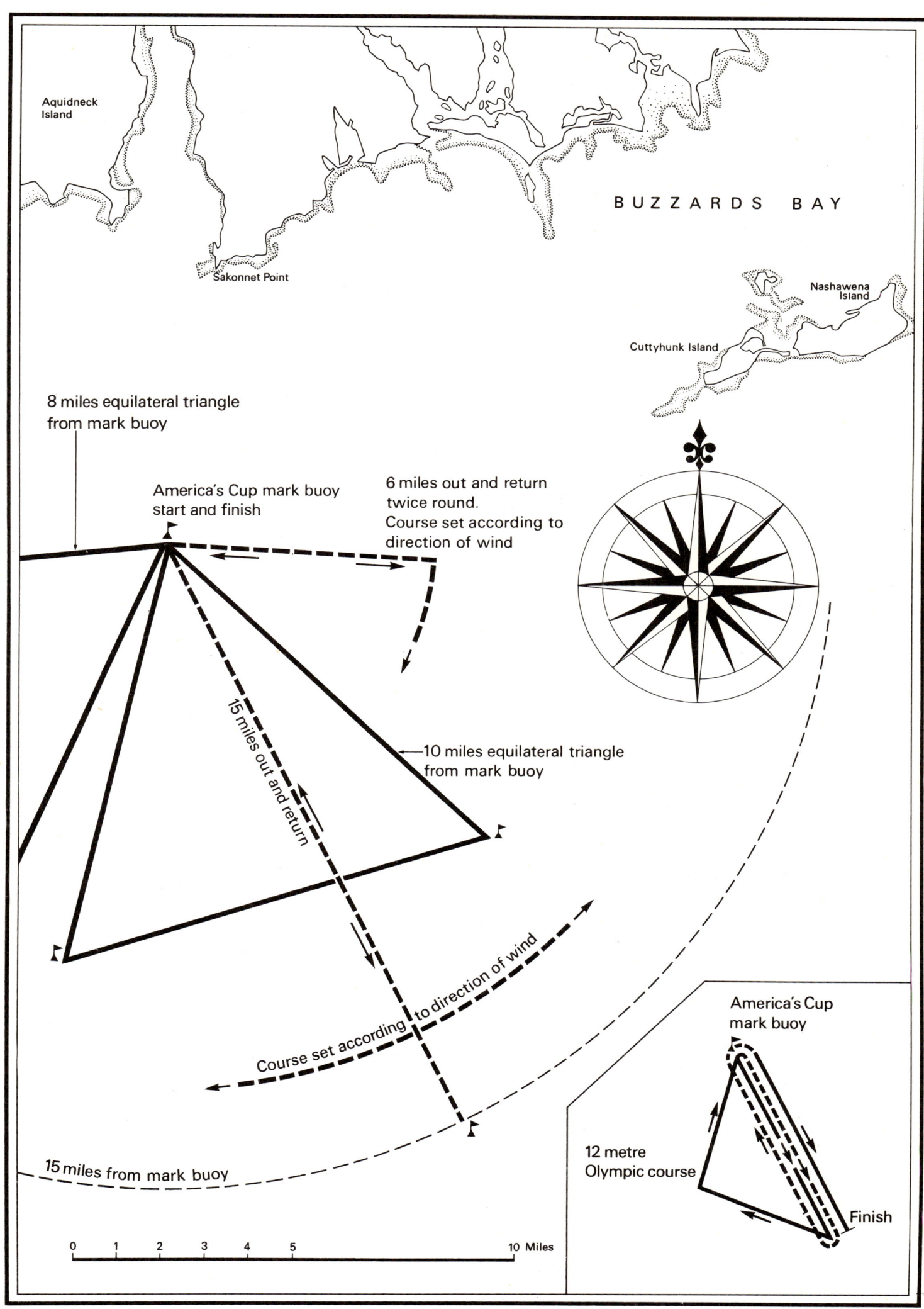

BUZZARDS BAY

Aquidneck Island

Sakonnet Point

Nashawena Island

Cuttyhunk Island

8 miles equilateral triangle from mark buoy

America's Cup mark buoy start and finish

6 miles out and return twice round. Course set according to direction of wind

15 miles out and return

10 miles equilateral triangle from mark buoy

Course set according to direction of wind

15 miles from mark buoy

America's Cup mark buoy

12 metre Olympic course

Finish

0 1 2 3 4 5   10 Miles

America's Cup Courses off Newport, Rhode Island 1930-1970

For all the courses shown on this chart, including the 12-metre Olympic course, the America's Cup mark buoy is located nine miles south-east of Brenton Reef.

Colour Plates

AMERICA
1851

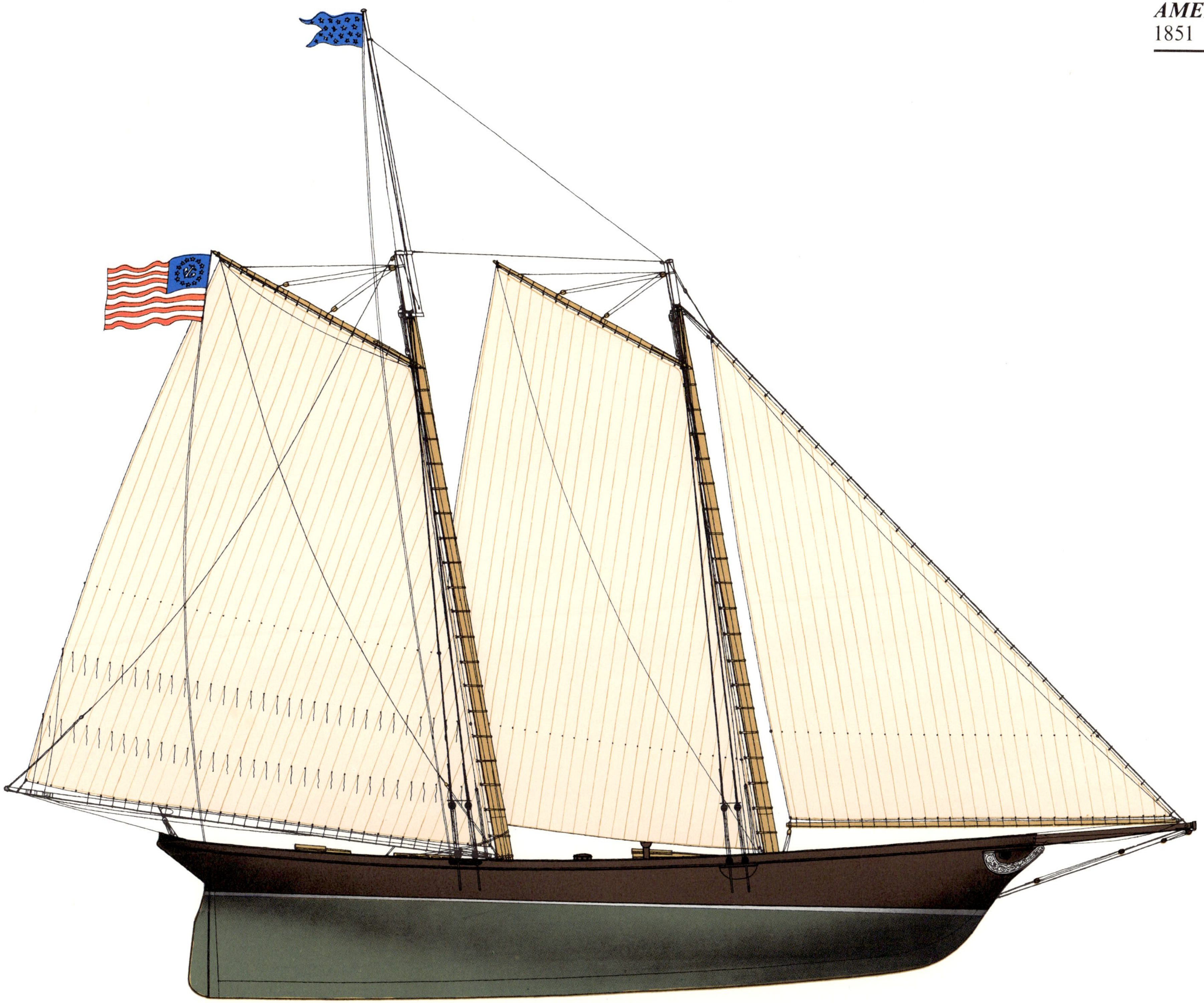

MAGIC
1870

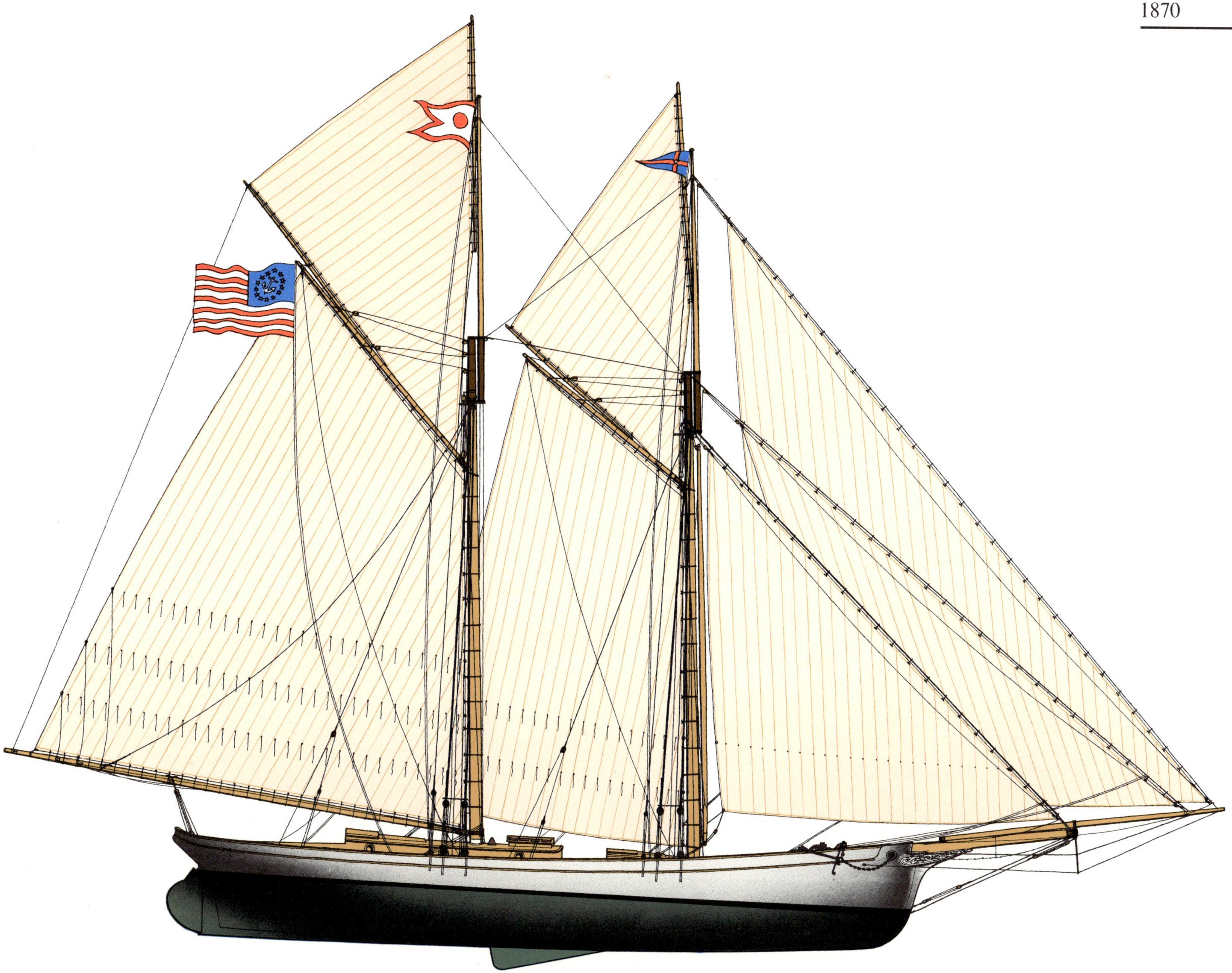

CAMBRIA
1870

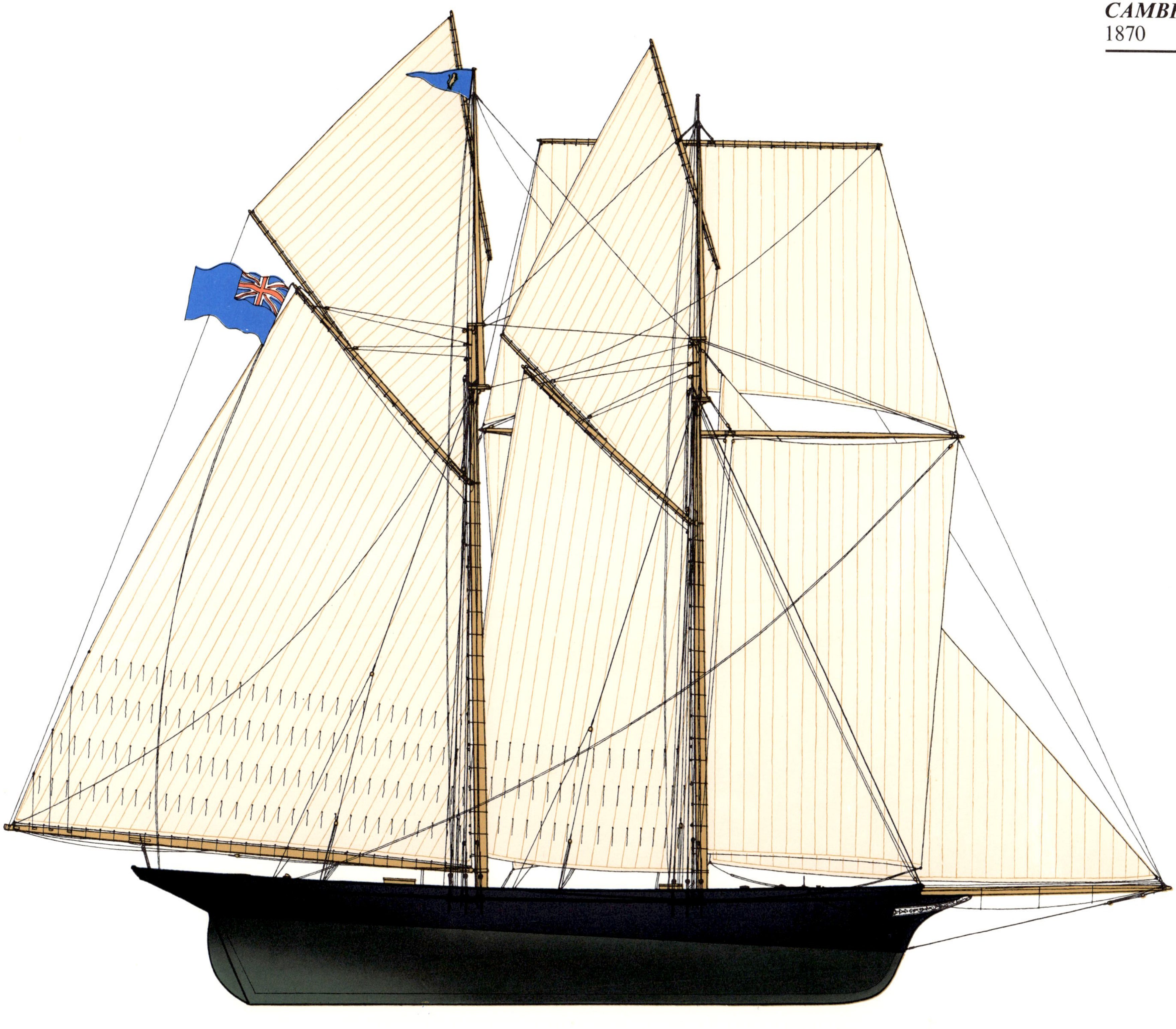

GENESTA
1885

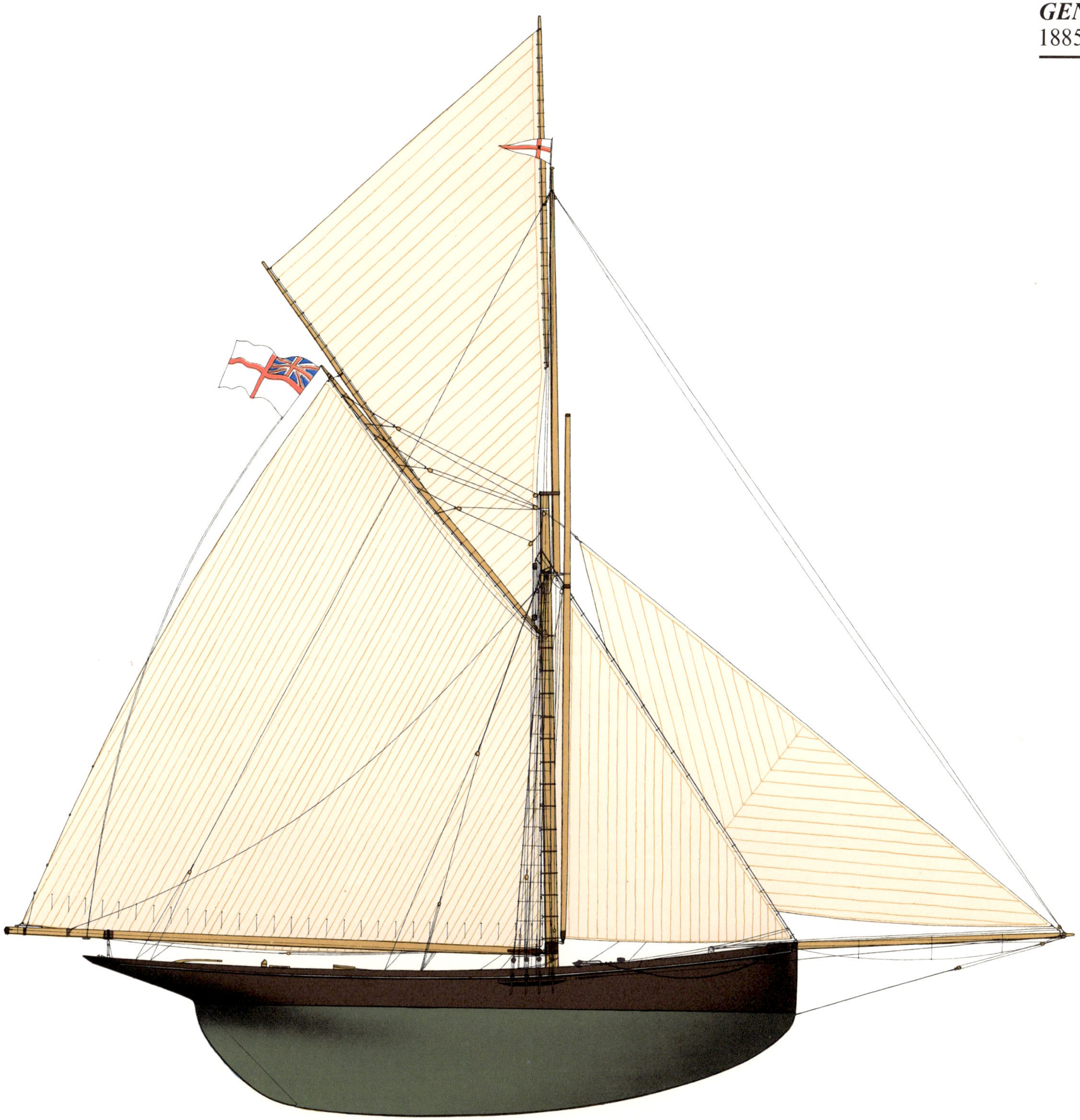

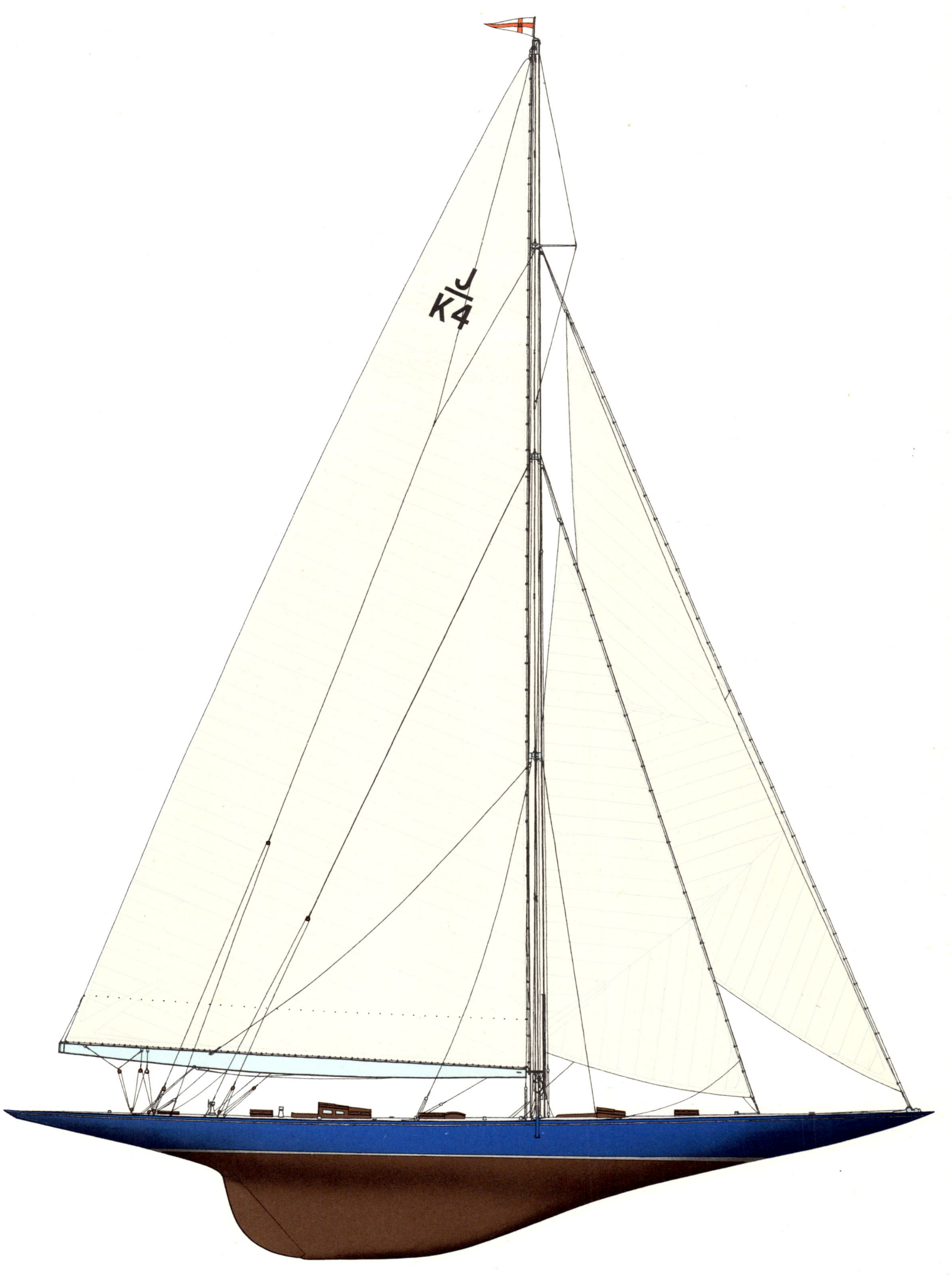

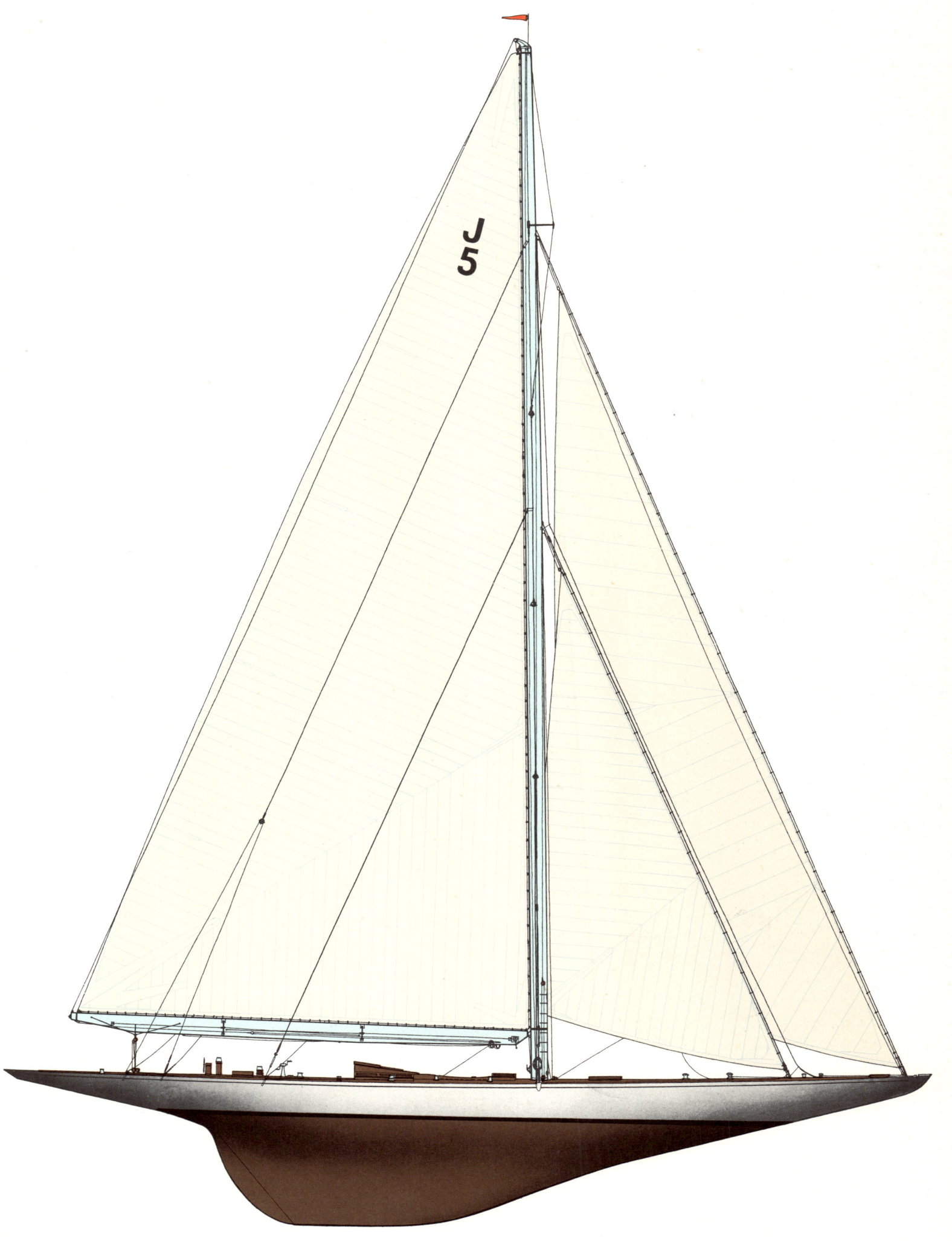

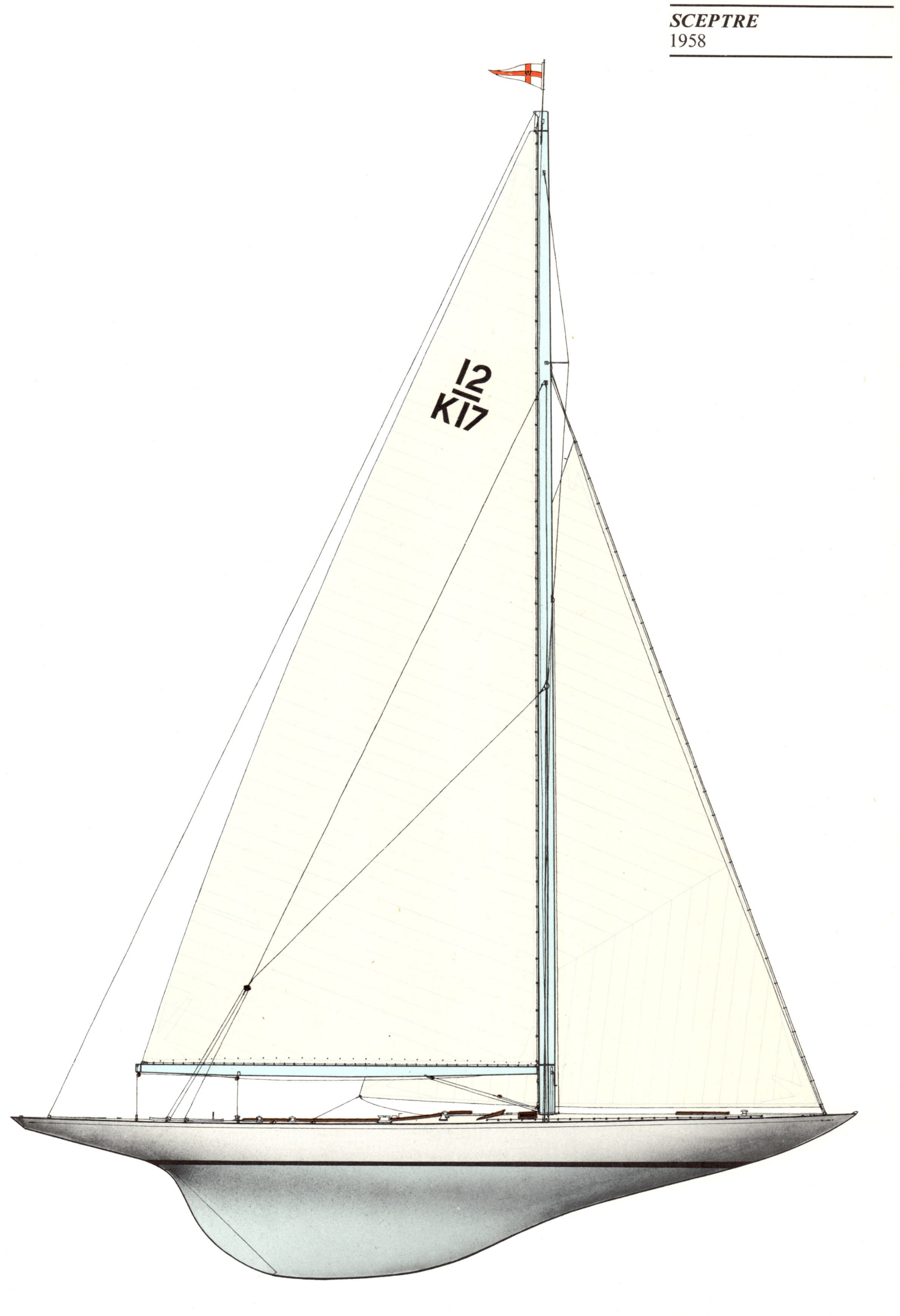

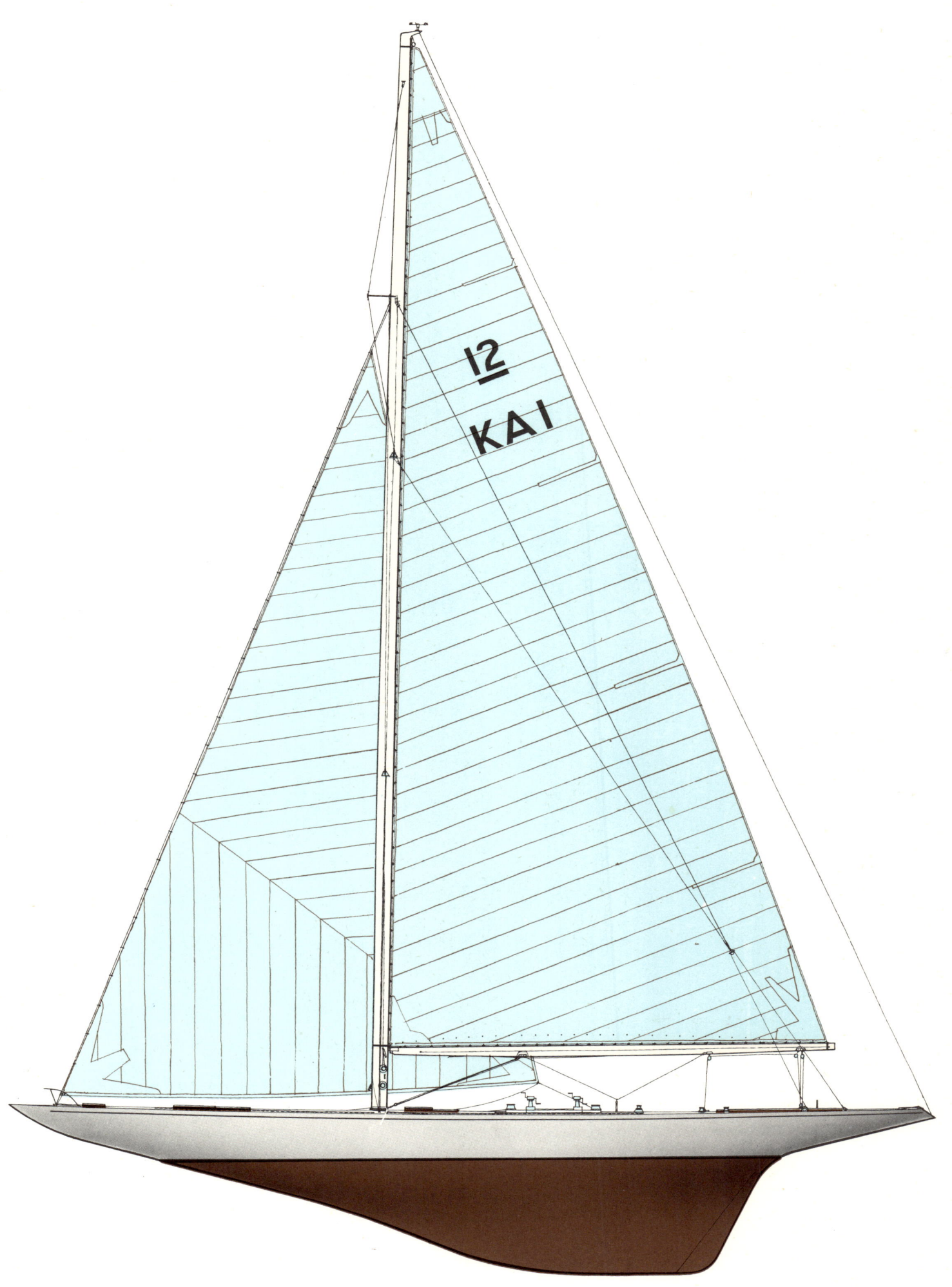

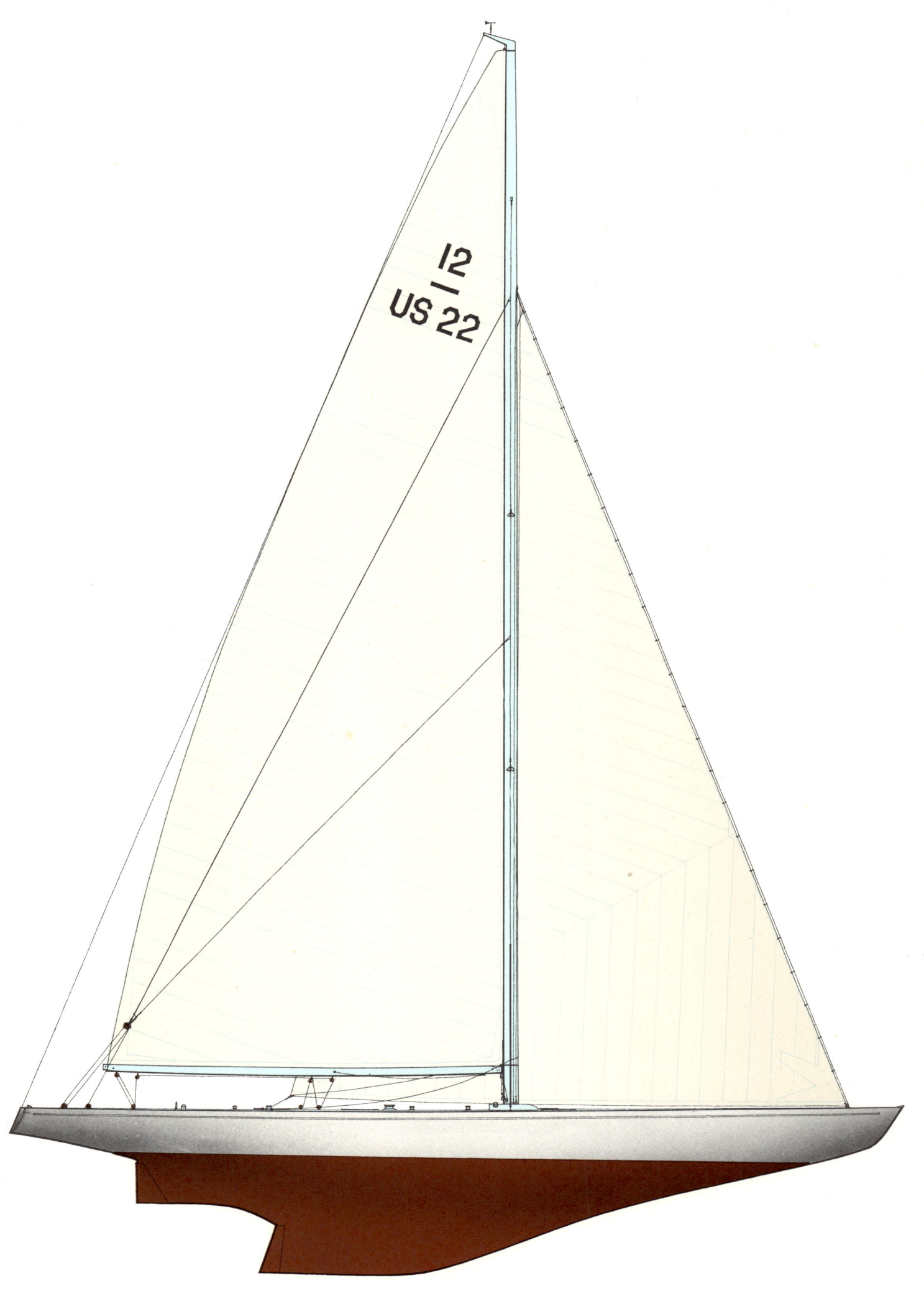